The Republican
Party in
American Politics

Charles O. Jones
THE UNIVERSITY OF ARIZONA

The Macmillan Company, New York
Collier–Macmillan Limited, London

TO VERA, JOE B., AND DANNIE, THREE OF THE
GREAT ONES.

First Printing

Library of Congress catalog card number: 65–15191

THE MACMILLAN COMPANY, NEW YORK
COLLIER–MACMILLAN CANADA, LTD., TORONTO, ONTARIO

PRINTED IN THE UNITED STATES OF AMERICA

The author is grateful to Rutgers University Press for granting
permission to quote from his book *Party and Policy-Making:
The House Republican Policy Committee,* copyright © 1965
by Rutgers—The State University.

Preface

As a Republican, I am interested in the development of my party. As a political scientist, I am interested in analyzing the function of the party of opposition in American politics. Nelson W. Polsby encouraged me to combine these interests by writing a book on the Republican Party which might serve to stimulate undergraduate students to think about some of the questions I have in mind. I have tried to accomplish this goal in the following book. The book focuses on the Republican Party in the contemporary political scene, but there are broad implications for the political system in an inquiry which seeks to explain the semipermanent minority role of the Republican Party. I have by no means discovered all the implications of this phenomenon in American politics, and I invite students to extend the inquiry.

In addition to expressing my gratitude to Nelson W. Polsby, who also read and improved the manuscript with careful editing, and Robert J. Patterson, political science editor for The Macmillan Company, I wish to acknowledge the assistance of several other friends. My colleague at the University of Arizona, Conrad Joyner, who knows a great deal about the subject matter of this book, also read the manuscript and was helpful in his criticisms and comments. Several people deserve credit for suffering me while I talked out the structure of the book. These include my wife, Vera, Harold Rhodes, Robert Carlile, Jorgen Rasmussen, and Rosendo Gomez. I also am indebted to John Kessel and Patricia Chase of the Republican National Committee, and Robert Berry for assisting in various ways.

The manuscript was typed by Miss Beverly Bigwood and Miss Shelly Harrell of the Department of Government and Institute of Government Research, University of Arizona. In addition to secretarial assistance, the Institute of Government Research supported me with a research grant for the Summer, 1964.

Finally, I want to draw special attention to those persons to whom this book is dedicated—my wife and sons. They make life worth living and books worth writing. They are truly three of the great ones.

Charles O. Jones

Contents

CHAPTER 1

The Republican Party—
An Introduction

THE MAJOR PURPOSE of this book is to introduce you to the Republican Party—one of America's two great political parties. It is primarily a description of that party in contemporary American politics—its organization, its leaders, its supporters, its problems, and its work. The book is more than straightforward description, however. It is an analysis of an opposition party, because the Republicans have been the minority party in national politics since 1932. In explaining Republican Party characteristics, I shall often make reference to the fact that it is the "second party" in American politics today. And I shall contend that there are differences in characteristics and functioning between majority parties and minority parties.

The book is organized to discuss what I consider to be the two major functions of a political party in any political system. There are certain fundamental prerequisites that must be met before a government can operate. First, there must be processes for selecting personnel to work in government. Second, there must be processes established so that government can attend to public problems. Parties are instruments for organizing these two types of processes. In democratic political systems, the personnel in major positions of responsibility are elected by the people. Thus, parties function to organize the electoral process. They recruit candidates, organize the nominating process, register voters, educate voters, transport voters to the polls, raise money, and organize campaigns. Without parties to do these things, it is hard to see how representative democracy in modern society could work.

Political parties in democracy also function to organize the policy-making process. Once their candidates have been elected, parties then designate leaders in policy-making institutions (primarily legislatures) and establish committees, procedures, and rules, to facilitate both the representation of those who want something from government (for example, interest groups) and the resolution of the conflicts that are the result of competing demands on government. Again, parties willingly assume the responsibility to organize this vast policy-making

1

process, though many people are justly critical of how effective political parties perform this function.[1]

To clarify further the function of political parties in the political system, it is useful to compare their functions with those of interest groups. Political parties are not primarily policy-oriented in the sense of being for or against specific solutions to public problems. They act as conduits for those groups and individuals who do have policy preferences and to that extent become oriented in the direction of one solution in preference to another, but they do not function to make policy demands for one alternative solution to another. Interest groups, on the other hand, are policy-oriented. They function to make demands—specific demands for specific solutions to specific public problems. On the whole they do not organize elections and policy-making, since with that responsibility comes the task of organizing a means for resolving conflict, for effecting compromise. An interest group does not want to compromise. It does not want to be responsible for providing mechanisms that will represent other interests, perhaps those in competition with its own. For example, I once heard an official of the AFL-CIO complain that his organization was too closely identified with the Kennedy Administration and the Democratic Party. The Democrats assumed they could depend on the support of the AFL-CIO. When the Kennedy Administration pressured them to endorse a compromise on a public housing issue, however, the AFL-CIO balked. They did not want to compromise. They wanted everything they could get in this particular policy area. In the opinion of this union official, developing compromises was the responsibility of the Democratic Party—not of the AFL-CIO.

In short, the political party organizes the government. The interest group makes demands of the government. Both groups are essential for the proper functioning of a democratic political system.

I am not saying that political parties do not become policy-oriented—only that it is not their primary function in the political system to make policy on public problems. Our two parties have

[1] There are many standard lists of party functions which are much more elaborate than the one I have presented here. Most of the items on more elaborate lists, I think, are subsidiary to organizing the electoral and policy-making processes. Thus, for example, Frank Sorauf mentions "political socialization" as a function of party. I agree but would argue that it performs this task as a part of organizing elections and policy-making. See Sorauf, *Political Parties in the American System* (Boston: Little, Brown, 1964), pp. 2–6.

long been identified with certain policy positions. Generally speaking, however, this identity is a result of the fact that certain interests have more access to one party than to the other. Thus, in domestic affairs, business groups have traditionally had more access to the Republican Party, and labor groups have had more access to the Democratic Party. There is no immutable law, however, that Republicans have to be oriented toward policy preferences favored by businessmen, and Democrats toward those favored by labor. In fact, certain Republican decision makers are oriented to labor, and certain Democrats are oriented to business. At certain times and in certain places each of the groups has had primary access to the other party.

Austin Ranney and Willmoore Kendall, among others, have discussed the problems of defining majority and minority parties; in some states the Republican Party is clearly the majority party, even though it is the minority party nationally.[2] Still, it is possible to speak of a *national majority party,* both in terms of the preferences among the voters and in terms of control of Congress and the Presidency. When one party is preferred by a majority of voters *and* controls Capitol Hill and the White House, that party is clearly the *majority* party. If there is a division among these variables (for example, the Democratic Party is preferred by a majority of voters but a Republican is in the White House), then the majority-minority situation is ambiguous. And when the majority-minority situation is ambiguous, there is less distinct differentiation between the two parties in regard to their functions in elections and policy-making.

During a period of one-party dominance—for example, Democrats since 1932—it is likely that there will be correspondence between the party preferred by the voters and the party in control in Washington. Between 1932 and 1964, there was ambiguity for just eight years, 1952–1960. At this writing there is definitely a majority party. The Survey Research Center reports that a majority of citizens eligible to vote prefer the Democratic Party (see Chapter 4). Both the White House and the two houses of Congress are firmly in the control of the Democratic Party.

[2] See Austin Ranney and Willmoore Kendall, *Democracy and the American Party System* (New York: Harcourt, Brace & World, 1956), Chs. 7 and 8. See also Joseph Schlesinger, "A Two-Dimensional Scheme for Classifying the States According to Degree of Inter-Party Competition," *American Political Science Review,* Vol. 49 (December, 1955), pp. 1121–1128, and Schlesinger, "The Structure of Competition for Office in the American States," *Behavioral Science,* Vol. 5 (July, 1960), pp. 197–210.

While both the majority and minority parties in a two-party system function to organize the electoral and policy-making processes, there will likely be differences in the segments of each process the two parties will organize. When one party is clearly dominant, the national majority party is primarily the party of *advocacy*. The majority party bears the principal responsibility for organizing a policy-making process that will bridge the gaps of the separation of powers. It is expected to advocate and initiate solutions to public problems.

The national minority party is primarily the party of *criticism*. It organizes opposition to what the majority party advocates and initiates. The major institutions for initiating policy—Congress and the Presidency—are controlled by the majority party and therefore that party is expected to initiate solutions to public problems.

This differentiation in the sectors of functioning between the two parties does not mean that the majority party is always innovative and the minority party is always negatively critical. In fact, Theodore Lowi argues that "innovation is a function of the minority party."[3] His interpretation is that innovation is a method for converting a minority into a majority position. There is no necessary correlation between advocacy and innovation nor between criticism and negativism. In advocating, the majority party may be offering the same solutions to problems that have been offered for decades. In criticizing, the minority party may be countering with solutions that are bold and innovative. The distinction between the two is principally one of which party is expected to advocate or initiate. The majority party has the initiative because it controls the government. It defines problems, decides which problems to attack, and whose demands will be favored. The minority party responds to this initiative.

Historical Development of the Republican Party

In his history of the Republican Party, Malcolm Moos states that "the paternity of the Republican party is an uncommonly complex matter."[4] Though it is not possible to identify all of the causes of

---

[3] Theodore Lowi, "Toward Functionalism in Political Science: The Case of Innovation in Party Systems," *American Political Science Review,* Vol. LVII (September, 1963), p. 571.

[4] Malcolm Moos, *The Republicans, A History of Their Party* (New York: Random House, 1956), p. 1. Much of this section relies on the work of Professor Moos. For other histories of the party, see the Bibliography, p. 148.

development of the party or their priority, it is possible to list the more important of them. And clearly central to the emergence of the Grand Old Party (GOP) was the passage of the Kansas-Nebraska Act in 1854. This Act rejected earlier compromises which excluded slavery from the Northwest Territory and provided that "it being the true intent and meaning of this act not to legislate slavery into any Territory or State, nor to exclude it therefrom, but to leave the people thereof perfectly free to form and regulate their domestic institutions in their own way, subject only to the Constitution of the United States."[5] This doctrine of "squatter sovereignty" upset political alignments across the nation. With incredible speed the "anti-Nebraska" mood was translated into victory at the polls in the North for those critical of the Act. That piece of legislation served as a catalyst to unify opinions, attitudes, and forces which had been extant for decades.

One of the several anti-Nebraska protest meetings to be held in 1854 was in a small schoolhouse in Ripon, Wisconsin. This meeting on March 20, 1854, followed an earlier meeting on March 1 in which a number of Whigs, Free Soilers, and Democrats threatened to form a new party if the Kansas-Nebraska bill passed the Senate. It passed the Senate on March 3. The threat was carried out in the March 20 meeting, and the Republican Party was born.[6]

Few democratic political parties in the world have had a more auspicious beginning than the Republican Party. In the congressional elections of 1854, months after the party had been first established, a majority of anti-Nebraskans were elected to the House of Representatives. Most of these were called "Americans" or "Know-Nothings," but approximately 40 were Republicans. In addition, several Republican Senators and Governors were elected. Still, as Malcolm Moos argues, the Republican Party was not firmly established as the

---

[5] *U. S. Statutes-At-Large,* Vol X (Boston: Little, Brown, 1855), p. 283.

[6] There has always been controversy as to the exact birthplace of the Republican Party. Both Ripon, Wisconsin, and Jackson, Michigan, claim the honor, as do several other communities. Jackson's claim is based on the fact that a formal meeting was held there on July 6, 1854. Thus they argue that the party really was formed on that date. Moos refers to an article by A. J. Turner—"The Genesis of the Republican Party," Wisconsin *State Register,* Portage, Wisconsin (March, 1898)—which makes the point that there were meetings held in many communities to protest the Kansas-Nebraska Act. The history of the party issued by the Republican National Committee compromises by referring to "The movement begun in the Ripon church *and* [our italics] 'under the oaks' at Jackson..."—*The History of the Republican Party* (Washington, D.C.: Republican National Committee, 1962), p. 10.

opposition party. The anti-Nebraska mood might still have taken any number of forms. The Republican Party had to organize and prove itself in the 1856 presidential election.

On June 17, 1856, following several preliminary meetings to organize a national Republican Party, the first Republican National Convention nominated as candidates former Senator John C. Fremont, California, for President and former Senator William L. Dayton, New Jersey, for Vice-President. The "Know-Nothing" Party, the Republicans' principal rival in assuming the role of opposition party, nominated former President Millard Fillmore and A. J. Donelson as candidates. The northern wing of the "Know-Nothings" split from the party and eventually endorsed the Republican ticket.

The results of the 1856 election clearly established the Republican Party as the second party, the opposition party, the party to represent the antislavery mood. The Democratic candidates, James Buchanan for President and John Breckinridge for Vice-President, won handily with 174 electoral votes, but the Republican candidates garnered 114 electoral votes and the "Know-Nothing" candidates only 8. Fremont carried 11 northern states, including New York state and all of New England. Buchanan won all the southern states and enough northern states to win. Fillmore carried only Maryland. Though the Democrats captured control of both the House and the Senate, the opposition was definitely centered in the Republican Party, rather than split among several political groups. As James Whittier wrote:

> If months have well-nigh won the field,
> What may not four years do?[7]

President Buchanan had only just moved into the White House when the Supreme Court handed down the momentous Dred Scott decision. Congress, the Court said, did not have the right to exclude slavery from new territories. Slaves were property, they were not citizens. This opinion, according to Professor Robert McCloskey, was "the most disastrous . . . the Supreme Court has ever issued."[8]

The Kansas-Nebraska Act, the Dred Scott decision, a proslavery constitution in Kansas—these and other events were the prelude to Democratic loss of the House of Representatives in 1858, loss of the Presidency and the House in 1860, and the Civil War in 1861.

---

[7] Quoted in Stefan Lorant, *The Presidency* (New York: Macmillan, 1952), p. 227.

[8] Robert McCloskey, *The American Supreme Court* (Chicago: University of Chicago Press, 1960), p. 94.

One Republican candidate for the Senate who did not win in 1858 was Abraham Lincoln of Illinois. He did not win enough votes in the state legislature (which then elected United States Senators), but he did win national recognition in the series of debates with Democratic incumbent Stephen Douglas. The Lincoln-Douglas debates were instrumental in "the making of the President, 1860."

The second Republican National Convention was held in Chicago on May 16, 1860, in a hastily constructed wooden structure called the Wigwam. Seven candidates for President were nominated, but only Senator William Seward of New York and Abraham Lincoln were serious contenders. Seward led the first two ballots, but Lincoln was to be the candidate. With the galleries packed for Lincoln and cheering loudly, delegation after delegation jumped on the bandwagon after Lincoln went over the top on the third ballot. Senator Hannibal Hamlin from Maine was the vice-presidential candidate.

The Democratic Party split in 1860 between the north and south. The northern Democrats nominated Senator Stephen Douglas and Senator Hershel Johnson from Georgia as candidates for President and Vice-President. The southern Democrats nominated Vice-President John Breckinridge from Kentucky and Senator Joseph Lane from Oregon. The remnants of the Whig and American parties formed the Constitutional Union Party and nominated as candidate for President Senator John Bell from Tennessee and for Vice-President, the great Massachusetts orator, preacher, professor, and legislator, Edward Everett.

The results of the election in 1860 are well known. Lincoln and Hamlin won all but 3 of the northern free states' electoral votes, a total of 180. Breckinridge and Lane garnered 72 electoral votes, all from the south. Bell and Everett won 3 border slave states, for a total of 39 electoral votes. Douglas and Johnson won only Missouri and 3 electoral votes in New Jersey, for a total of 12. This was sectionalism run rampant, but Lincoln was able to win a majority. His victory was the catalyst to violent action—the spark to ignite a fire which had smoldered for so long.

There is no need to discuss the details of the Civil War. Suffice it to say that the Republican Party became the party of national unity and freedom for the slaves. Although it suffered periodic losses, the Republican Party emerged from the 1860's as the dominant political party in America and remained so until 1930. A Democratic presidential victory during this period was a deviation—the result of internal Republican party splits or economic disturbances in the country.

Often despite lackluster candidates and programs, the Republicans were able to win.[9]

The extent of Republican dominance is easily demonstrated. Between 1860 and 1932 (72 years and 18 presidential terms), the Democrats controlled the White House for just 16 years, 4 presidential terms (discounting Andrew Johnson's takeover following Lincoln's assassination), although they came close to winning on a number of occasions—for example, in 1876, 1880, and 1888. During this period just two Democratic Presidents were elected, Grover Cleveland and Woodrow Wilson (each for two terms), and 11 Republican Presidents were elected. The Democrats did somewhat better in Congress because they developed ironclad control over House and Senate seats in the South following Reconstruction. Still the Republicans dominated. Of the 36 congressional sessions between 1860 and 1932, the Republicans controlled 23 House sessions and 31 Senate sessions.

The period of Republican Party dominance was a period during which America developed maturity as a nation. Despite periodic setbacks, the country expanded in every way. Fourteen states were admitted between 1860 and 1932; many of these were to become strong Republican states.[10] Agricultural production increased phenomenally. Capital investment in machinery, workingmen's wages, real and personal wealth, transportation—all increased by incredible proportions. Though it can hardly be argued that the Republican Party was responsible for the industrial revolution in America, it can be argued that it was this revolution's political beneficiary.

The Republican Party seemed to have achieved new heights of success in the 1920's. Little did any one realize that Herbert Hoover

[9] Few historians would claim that the Republican Party produced many great leaders during this period of history. Among its Presidents, only Abraham Lincoln, William McKinley, and Theodore Roosevelt receive plaudits. There were some—for example, Ulysses S. Grant and Warren G. Harding—that even Republicans would like to forget. In fact, many Republican candidates who lost, 1932—1952, might well be classed as superior to those who won before 1932.

[10] The states which entered were Kansas, 1861; Nevada, 1864; Nebraska, 1867; Colorado, 1876; North Dakota, South Dakota, Montana, and Washington, 1889; Wyoming and Idaho, 1890; Utah, 1896; Oklahoma, 1907; and Arizona and New Mexico, 1912. Of these, all but two, Idaho and Oklahoma, gave their electoral votes to the Republican presidential candidate in a Majority of the presidential elections between their admittance to the Union and 1932. Idaho voted Republican five times, Democratic four, and Populist once. Oklahoma voted Democratic four times and Republican twice.

would be the last Republican President for twenty years. Hoover won a smashing victory in 1928. He carried 40 states, including such states as Florida, Kentucky, North Carolina, Oklahoma, Tennessee, Texas, Virginia, and West Virginia. Hoover was called the "Wonder Boy" and Republicans looked forward to many more years as the majority party in American politics.

The collapse was dramatic. Within a few months of his inauguration, on October 24, 1929, President Hoover was faced with the greatest economic crisis in the history of the American Republic. Though not so apparent at the time, the Republican Party's era of dominance was crumbling along with the stock market. Nearly sixty-nine years after the Civil War had resulted in the emergence, with strength, of a new political party, an equally cataclysmic event again upset the political balance. Professor E. E. Schattschneider summarizes what had happened: "The election of 1932 was much more than the defeat of a political party; it was something very much like the overthrow of a ruling class."[11] The beneficiary on this occasion was the Democratic Party. In the congressional elections of 1930, the Republicans lost 49 seats in the House and 8 Senate seats. But 1930 was relative victory for Republicans compared to what was to happen in the next six years.

In 1928 Hoover carried 40 states; in 1932 he carried 6. In 1928 there were 267 Republicans in the House of Representatives; in 1932 there were 117. In 1928 there were 56 Republican Senators; in 1932 there were 36. And the Democratic juggernaut was to continue. In 1936, Republican Presidential Candidate, Alfred M. Landon of Kansas, carried only two states, Maine and Vermont, with 8 electoral votes. The number of House Republicans was reduced to 103 in 1934 and to *89* in 1936. The number of Republican Senators fell to 25 in 1934 and to *17* in 1936. To this day the Republican Party has not recovered from what Schattschneider has termed "the largest displacement of conflicts in American history . . ."[12]—a reference to the fact that economic, political, and social behavior was drastically altered by the Depression.

After 1930, the Republican Party had to adjust to a new role in American politics—the role of the minority party. It was aided in effecting a rapid adjustment by successive defeats at the polls in 1932, 1934, and 1936. There was no doubt in the minds of Republicans

[11] E. E. Schattschneider, *The Semi-Sovereign People* (New York: Holt, Rinehart, & Winston, 1960), p. 86.
[12] Schattschneider, p. 89.

by 1936 that they now belonged to the minority party and that this status was not an aberration of one election. The Republican Party did not collapse, however. It says something for the maturation of our two-party system that despite these stunning defeats, the Republican Party remained a strong and vital force in American politics—garnering nearly 38 per cent of the two-party popular vote for President on that bleak November day in 1936.

When a party does not control the White House, the Congress becomes its home—its retreat. And for twenty years, the center of the Republican Party, in its public policy-making role, was on Capitol Hill. During the depths of the Republican Party's political depression, 1934–1938, congressional Republicans simply stood aside and let the Roosevelt steamroller pass by. Even in 1937, when President Roosevelt decided to press his advantage by adjusting the separation of powers with his unpopular proposal to increase the size of the Supreme Court, Senate Minority Leader Charles McNary and his sixteen followers adopted the "operation silence" strategy. "Let the boys across the aisle do the talking" was McNary's advice.[13]

By 1939, congressional Republicans, buoyed up by an increase of 80 seats in the House and 6 seats in the Senate, could afford to adopt a more belligerent strategy. Though Roosevelt continued to plague them by defeating Republican presidential candidates, congressional Republicans were gradually winning seats that had been lost during the Depression. Republicans were very much encouraged by their gain of 5 seats in the Senate in 1940 and ecstatic about a 10-seat increase (to 38) in 1942. In the House, they lost only 7 seats in 1940 and gained 47 in 1942. Their victories were checked in 1944 when their old nemesis, President Roosevelt, captured a fourth term, but in 1946, for the first time in sixteen years, the Republicans controlled both the House and the Senate. With the death of Roosevelt, the end of the war, the unpopularity of President Harry S. Truman, a split in the Democratic Party, their great victories in 1946, and, in Republican eyes, a fine record in the Eightieth Congress, Republicans had every right to look forward to an end of the drought in 1948. They would once again reestablish themselves in their rightful role in American politics as the party of advocacy—of leadership.

The story of the 1948 election has been told in many books, analyses of polls, errant headlines (the *Chicago Tribune's* early edition announced "Dewey Defeats Truman"); but no version can fully

13 Moos, pp. 406–407.

capture the effect of that poll on the Republican Party. Everyone had assured Republicans of victory—everyone but Harry Truman. Yet they suffered a complete rout. Though the upset of New York's Governor Thomas E. Dewey was the focus of attention, he was not the only Republican defeated in 1948. After painfully struggling for sixteen years to fashion majorities in the House and Senate, Republicans lost 75 seats in the House and 9 seats in the Senate—their worst congressional defeat since 1932.

After gains in 1950, Republican fortunes appeared to be on the rise in 1952, although no one dared be too optimistic. As millions sat in their living rooms and stared into a little box called "television," the party placed its internal divisions on public display in its 1952 convention. The "modern" Republican candidate was a newcomer to the political scene. Republicans had tried the tactic of nominating a new face in 1940 with Wendell L. Willkie and failed. Many Republicans argued that with victory so close at hand, the party should nominate its "Mr. Conservative Republican"—Senator Robert A. Taft of Ohio. Others argued, however, that "Mr. Republican" could not win and the party should take no chances of an upset in 1952. The "others" won the day and nominated General Dwight D. Eisenhower. Their analysis seemed vindicated by the election results since the General proved to be the greatest vote-getter in the history of the Republican Party.

Republicans had cause to be jubilant after the 1952 election. They had captured both prizes—the White House and Congress. At the same time, the old "pros" knew that the "good old days" still had not returned. Despite Eisenhower's great personal triumph, Republicans had only an 8-seat majority in the House and a 1-seat majority in the Senate. One writer was moved to inquire, *Is There a Republican Majority?*[14] The triumph for the Republican Party did not match the triumph of General Eisenhower; this fact was demonstrated in 1954, 1956, and 1958, when congressional Republicans sustained successive losses. By 1960, there were only 154 Republicans in the House (the fewest since 1937–1938) and 34 in the Senate (the fewest since 1941–1942).

In summary, the Republican Party catapulted to success shortly after its founding in 1854. It benefited from the disunity caused by the most divisive issue in American history. The party capitalized on its advantage and organized as a strong national party that dom-

[14] Louis Harris, *Is There a Republican Majority?* (New York: Harper, 1954).

inated American politics for seventy years. The fall came as swiftly as the rise. Republicans were demolished at the polls because they were held responsible for the economic crisis of the early 1930's. The party of advocacy became the party of criticism and it remains so today. It is that party of criticism that I shall be describing in the following chapters.

Part I

The Republican Party and Elections

CHAPTER 2

Organizing Republicans

DESCRIBING PARTY ORGANIZATION in American politics is an extremely difficult endeavor. The term *organization* implies system, pattern, neatness. The symbol of organization is the pyramid—many subunits responsible to various intermediate units that are responsible to a single unit at the top. This "hierarchy of authority" conception of organization is of very little assistance in describing and understanding American party organization. Indeed, if organization is defined as hierarchy of authority, then it would be appropriate to employ another term in describing American parties—perhaps *party apparatus*. I will employ the term *organization,* but it should be noted at the outset that it simply refers to the party apparatus—its committees, leaders, conventions, headquarters—and not to any specific, predetermined relationships within that apparatus (for example, a hierarchy of authority).

The late V. O. Key, Jr., described American parties as a "system of layers of organization."[1] Other students of parties are content to observe that our parties are decentralized. However described, the fact is that both parties have a multiplicity of organizations throughout the United States and that there are few occasions when all of the various units are integrated and coordinated for achieving a common goal. Collecting all of the various state, local, and national party agencies and getting them to move in the same direction at the same time is a supreme challenge.

Critics of the American party system point a moralistic finger at American party disorganization and shout for reform. Often it seems that these critics are suggesting that the parties are decentralized by some sinister design. In fact, American political parties have organized themselves in accordance with the way the American political system is organized. Federalism, separation of powers, staggered elections—these are the characteristics of the American political system.[2] Elections are frequent and many positions of authority are

---

[1] V. O. Key, Jr., *Politics, Parties, and Pressure Groups* (5th ed.; New York: Crowell, 1964), p. 316.

[2] See section entitled "Why American Parties Are as They Are," in Austin Ranney and Willmoore Kendall, *Democracy and the American Party System* (New York: Harcourt, Brace & World, 1956), pp. 493–504.

elective positions. There is only one national elective office—the Presidency—and the existence of that office may well hold the national party together. Other elections take place in every state, county, city, village, township, and hamlet across the nation. If a major function of political parties is to organize elections, then we should expect parties to organize where the elections are. If they organize where elections are, the parties are bound to be characterized by decentralized organization. In brief, it is too much to expect that the party system will be centrally organized when the election system is not.

There are several levels of party organization in the United States and there are also several party units at any one level. The most general classification of party units at the national, state, or local levels distinguishes between units primarily concerned with elections and those primarily concerned with policy-making. The former will be referred to as comprising the *extragovernmental party organization;* the latter as the *governmental party organization.* Most of the attention in this chapter will be on the extragovernmental party organization.

The lack of integration between the various levels of party organization means that a description of how Republicans organize for national elections is bound to be untidy. Though it is possible to describe various organizational units at the national level—the national committee, the national headquarters, the national convention—it is not possible to ascribe to those units the sole responsibility for organizing national elections. State and local units share this responsibility. If they are strong, they take whatever share they want; they are virtually autonomous in their relationship with the national organization. Thus, when I state that it is the function of political parties to organize elections, it does not imply that this function will be performed efficiently by a central organization. In the United States, this function is performed at many different levels by many different organizational units, with minimal coordination between the units.

During national elections, the national organization makes a valiant effort to coordinate campaign activities and to serve state and local party organizations. Between elections the national party units prepare for the next major electoral event by doing research, issuing press releases, raising money, and making preparations for the nominating convention. Throughout it all, the National Chairman and the National Headquarters (the "permanent" party) have the suspicion that they are not really needed, that they serve no definable purpose. They have little money to dispense, their advice is not often wanted or accepted by state organizations, and their press releases are usually published but reach the front page of the newspaper only if other news is scarce. All in all, the extragovernmental national party organization is destined to be frustrated. The fact is that this organization is the institutionalization of the myth that there *is* a national party. The National Headquarters cannot be disbanded, even though no one is certain of its function, because that would be tantamount to admitting that there is no national party. (And there is some doubt that the national party structure even has the power to disband itself.) Thus, there is a National Committee, a National Chairman, and a National Headquarters, all of which "shake and move."[3]

It is particularly important for the minority party to have a national organization. The majority party can be more continuously aware of its national existence, since it has a definite leader—the President.

National Party Organization

The extragovernmental national Republican organization is principally centered in the National Headquarters—the national party's bureaucracy. There is of course a National Convention, but it meets only once in four years and then for the very special purpose of selecting presidential and vice-presidential nominees. There is a National Committee, but it meets infrequently during the year and is composed of individuals with uneven party credentials. Cotter and Hennessy refer to it as a "non thing."[4] There is a National Committee Chairman, but normally he is not a full-time chairman, and there is a high degree of turnover among chairmen in both parties. Thus, the day-to-day national party organization—the party organi-

---

[3] Cornelius P. Cotter and Bernard C. Hennessy, in *Politics Without Power: The National Party Committees* (New York: Atherton Press, 1964) note that a "major purpose of the National Committee is to survive." (See p. 8.) That is, the committee, its staff, and chairman, are all necessary to provide continuity, the nucleus for campaign organizations, and, most importantly, a symbol testifying to the fact that the party does exist. Thus, the National Committee and its supporting organization must survive so that the party itself will survive. The specific tasks of the national party organization are supportive of this major function. The organization will raise money, plan the national convention, issue press releases, assist local party organizations, engage in research.

[4] Cotter and Hennessy, p. 11.

zation that a Republican can actually "go to"—is the party's Head-quarters. For this reason, I have reversed the conventional method of discussing national party organization and shall examine the National Committee Headquarters first, the National Committee Chairman second, and the National Committee third.

Republican National Committee Headquarters

Theoretically, the National Committee represents the National Convention, and the National Headquarters is to assist the National Committee and its Chairman in their work. In fact, though there are frequent reorganizations that prevent the growth of a permanent "establishment," the Headquarters is forced to carry on with only the broadest policy direction from the National Committee. Their policy-making latitude will depend upon who is chairman, but even with the most forceful chairman, individual party bureaucrats find that they must make policy decisions in their day-to-day activities. And many of those in the party Headquarters would complain that they are more hampered than aided in their work by other party agencies (for example, the National Committee, the Convention, and volunteer groups).

National party bureaucracy is a rather recent development. Cotter and Hennessy record that the Republican National Committee had a Research Division in the 1920's. In 1936, the Research Division and other staff personnel of the Committee were located at 718 Jackson Place, a small building on Lafayette Square, just north of the White House. After several moves between 1936 and their first presidential victory in twenty years, the National Committee finally settled into the second floor of the Cafritz Building, 1625 I Street, N.W. They are still located at that address.[5] The National Committee Head-quarters has grown from three or four employees in the early days to as many as 350 during presidential campaigns; approximately 100 at other times.

Republican Headquarters' staffs have been characterized by frequent turnover, job insecurity, and, often, low morale. Though professionalization among party bureaucracies has developed rapidly in the last twenty-five years, the notion that a political party needs a bureaucracy has not been accepted by the public to the extent that

[5] Cotter and Hennessy, p. 5. See also Hugh A. Bone, *Party Committees and National Politics* (Seattle: University of Washington Press, 1958), Ch. 2.

detailed personnel procedures, such as those for the civil service, have as yet been worked out for party employees.

I have stated that the usual principles of organization do not apply to the national party organization. They do not apply to the national party Headquarters either. The Headquarters' precise structure is too ephemeral: its responsibilities are unclear and change frequently; its personnel roster is unstable. The Republican National Headquarters has ordinarily made no attempt to construct an organizational flow chart because any such chart would be deceptive, might well result in animosity between staff members, and certainly would be out of date as soon as the ink dried. All that can be offered here is a description of Headquarters organization as it existed at the time of the writing of this book—with a warning that changes are frequent.[6]

In 1964, aside from Chairman William Miller, a part-time chairman who also served as a Congressman from New York, two men in particular were important in the Headquarters organization—William S. Warner and Albert B. (AB) Hermann. Warner, an experienced political professional, was Staff Director of the Republican Congressional Campaign Committee between 1951 and 1961. Under William Miller he served as Executive Director of the National Committee. If there is a second in command in the Headquarters, it is the Executive Director. It is his responsibility to make decisions in the Chairman's absence. Warner also acted as Comptroller for the National Headquarters. In this capacity he was involved in budgeting and raising funds for the National Committee. In 1962, Warner suggested experimenting with a program to solicit contributions of ten dollars or more from the "average Republican rather than the 'fat cat' who has traditionally loomed large in American political finance."[7] Those who contributed received a membership card and a subscription to *Battle-Line,* the National Committee's biweekly publication. The initial response was encouraging enough so that larger mass mailings were tried. The results were that $700,000 was raised in 1962 and over $1,000,000 in 1963. The "sustaining membership"

---

[6] For example, following Goldwater's nomination and the selection of Dean Burch as National Committee Chairman, the National Headquarters underwent extensive reorganization. Many of those discussed here were reassigned, demoted, or fired. See *Congressional Quarterly Weekly Report,* September 25, 1964, pp. 2221–2229, for details.

[7] This quote is taken from an undated memorandum issued in 1964 by the Republican National Committee entitled, "Republican National Committee Sustaining Membership Program: A Successful Experiment in Party Finance."

program is now an important source of funds for the Republican National Committee.

AB Hermann directed the Political Organization Division under Chairman Miller. Hermann fully deserves the title "Mr. Republican Organization," since he probably knows more about the development of the national party bureaucracy and its relationship to other party units than any one else. He has served the Republican National Committee in some capacity since 1949. During much of that time he was also Administrative Assistant to Senator H. Alexander Smith of New Jersey. A number of subdivisions were included in Hermann's Political Organization Division. One of the most active in recent years has been the Southern Division, headed by I. Lee Potter in 1964. It represents the effort of the National Committee to win in the South. "Operation Dixie," as the effort is called, has had continuous financial support and can point to a number of victories in recent years at all levels—local and state offices, congressional seats, and presidential electors. The other active subdivisions in the Political Organization Division in 1964 were Minorities, headed by Clay Claiborne, a veteran Negro newspaperman; Labor; Agriculture; Nationalities; Senior Citizens; Veterans; Registration of Voters; Arts and Sciences, headed by a university professor on a fellowship from the National Center for Education in Politics; and Political Education and Training, a new subdivision, headed by Raymond Humphreys, whose job it was to develop more effective precinct organization. Humphreys, an experienced troubleshooter, acted in this capacity for the National Headquarters and the Capitol Hill party committees.

The other major divisions under Chairman Miller were less elaborate in organization. The Director of Public Relations, William B. Sprague, Jr., in 1964, had the unenviable responsibility of trying to get press, radio, and television coverage for the minority party. The Speaker's Bureau arranges for Republicans to speak to various groups, principally those which submit requests. The Research Division is generally acknowledged to be a most thorough and expert unit, more so than its counterpart in the Democratic National Headquarters. The bulk of the research activity falls into three categories: issues of public policy; personalities in politics; and elections, voting behavior, and public opinion. Dr. William Prendergast headed this division under Chairman Miller. He had considerable prestige both within the party and outside. His division also served congressional party groups from time to time.

Women are well represented at the National Headquarters. The Women's Division was headed by the Assistant Chairman of the National Committee, Mrs. Elly Peterson in 1964. It works primarily with women who are active in politics—candidates for office or leaders of state and local organizations. In addition, there is a National Federation of Republican Women. The Federation is an organization of volunteers that maintains its headquarters at the National Headquarters. It has an elected president, Mrs. Dorothy A. Elston in 1964, meets in biennial conventions, and issues its own publications and public relations materials. Traditionally, there has been rivalry between the Women's Division and the Federation.

Another "auxiliary" group is the Young Republican National Federation. It also holds conventions, selects its own leadership, and issues publications. The YGOP is organized in all fifty states and in certain states, notably California, has been the center of controversy.[8]

In 1964, as in other presidential election years, there was an Executive Director of the Republican National Convention. Miss Josephine Good, also the Executive Secretary of the Republican National Committee, served in this responsible capacity. She was in charge of coordinating all of the physical planning for the convention.

This is the National Party Headquarters. It is organized rather loosely to accomplish the ill-stated and fuzzy goals of the national party organization. Frequent reorganization, a high rate of turnover of personnel, lack of stability, all characterize the party's national bureaucracy. Yet since its inception, the party Headquarters has become increasingly important as the permanent working unit of the national party and it is likely that its functions will increase in the next decades. Gradually there is developing a corps of professionals who do survive reorganizations that follow changes in party leadership and are willing to suffer the instability, insecurity, and indignities of an emerging national party apparatus.

The National Chairman[9]

The National Chairman is formally selected by the National Committee to lead the extragovernmental party organization. There are a

---

[8] See Cotter and Hennessy, pp. 150–156 and Bone, pp. 50–58, for discussions of women's and YGOP activities.

[9] Cotter and Hennessy have two excellent chapters (Chs. 4 and 5) on the National Chairman.

number of important considerations in the selection of the chairman. First and foremost, if the party has a man in the White House, then the party Chairman must be acceptable to the President. During the Eisenhower Administration there were five chairmen (see Table 2–1) —all of whom had to be approved by the President. Second, the Chairman must be acceptable to the party's presidential candidate. Thus, it is often the case there is a changeover in chairmen as soon as the national convention has made its choice of presidential candidate. In 1964, Senator Goldwater selected one of his top aides, Dean Burch of Tucson, Arizona, to be Chairman. Burch's assignment was to transform the National Headquarters into a Goldwater campaign organization. Finally, when the party does not control the White House and has not as yet selected a presidential candidate, the leading figures in the party are instrumental in deciding who will be chairman. For example, following Senator Thruston Morton's resignation as National Chairman in 1961, party leaders such as former President Dwight D. Eisenhower, defeated presidential candidate Richard M. Nixon, Senate Minority Leader Everett M. Dirksen of Illinois, House Minority Leader Charles A. Halleck of Indiana, Governor Nelson A. Rockefeller of New York, Senator Barry M. Goldwater of Arizona, and Senator Morton himself were among those who participated in the decision to select William E. Miller. It is in this latter situation that the most bitter battles are likely to take place. Thus, in 1949, following the stunning defeat of Governor Dewey at the hands of President Truman, National Chairman Hugh D. Scott, a Dewey supporter, was reelected by the National Committee by a narrow 4-vote majority after three days of "recrimination and name-calling."[10] Scott later resigned, in August, 1949, and a Taft man, Guy G. Gabrielson, was chosen.

The Chairman's duties are rather ill-defined and depend upon a variety of circumstances. Cotter and Hennessy refer to him as "a thousand-fingered Dutch boy." Former Chairman Meade Alcorn has described him as "the least appreciated, most abused, and most harassed party official in the country."[11] During elections he must concern himself with fund-raising. He often is the presidential candidate's campaign manager, although in 1960 this was not the case for either party's candidate. He must try to convince all of the multitudinous state and local organizations to work together for all Republican

---

[10] Malcolm Moos, *The Republicans, A History of Their Party* (New York: Random House, 1956), p. 450.
[11] Cotter and Hennessy, p. 63.

candidates, not just for local candidates. It is his responsibility to
effect coordination among regular party organizations and the various
national volunteer groups that emerge during presidential elections.
Professor Hugh A. Bone also refers to a "harmonizer" function
whereby the Chairman must try to mollify all the various elements in
the Republican Party.[12]

Between elections the Chairman's functions depend upon whether
there is a Republican in the White House. If so, then the Chairman
does whatever the President wants him to do. Generally, his duties
will include fund-raising, some patronage responsibilities, handling

Table 2–1. Republican National Committee Chairmen, 1930–1964

Chairman	Tenure	Major Political Experience
Simeon D. Fess, Ohio	1930–1932	U.S. Representative, 1913–1923; U.S. Senator, 1923–1925; Chairman, Republican National Congressional Committee, 1918–1922.
Everett Sanders, Indiana	1932–1934	U.S. Representative, 1917–1925; Republican National Committee staff, 1924; Secretary to President Coolidge, 1925–1929.
Henry P. Fletcher, Pennsylvania	1934–1936	Minister and Ambassador to Cuba, 1910–1916; Ambassador to Mexico, 1916–1920; Undersecretary of State, 1921–1922; Ambassador to Belgium, 1922–1924; Ambassador to Italy, 1924–1929.
John D. Hamilton, Kansas	1936–1940	State legislator, 1925–1928; Kansas State Party Chairman, 1932–1940; Member, Republican National Committee, 1932–1936.
Joseph W. Martin, Jr., Massachusetts	1940–1942	U.S. Representative, 1925–present; Speaker of the House of Representatives, 1947–1949, 1953–1955.
Harrison Spangler, Iowa	1942–1944	Iowa State Party Chairman, 1930–1932; Member of the Republican National Committee, 1931–1942.
Herbert Brownell, Jr., New York	1944–1946	State legislator, 1933–1937; Campaign Manager, Dewey for Governor, 1942; Attorney General of the U.S., 1953–1957.

[12] Bone, pp. 9–10.

Table 2–1. (continued)

Chairman	Tenure	Major Political Experience
B. Carroll Reece, Tennessee	1946–1948	U.S. Representative, 1921–1931, 1933–1947, 1951–1961.
Hugh D. Scott, Jr., Pennsylvania	1948–1949	U.S. Representative, 1941–1945, 1947–1959; U.S. Senator, 1959–present.
Guy G. Gabrielson, New Jersey	1949–1952	State legislator, 1926–1930; Member of the Republican National Committee.
Arthur Summerfield, Michigan	1952–1953	Finance Director, Michigan State Central Committee, 1943–1945; Member of Republican National Committee, 1944–1952; Postmaster General of the U.S., 1953–1961.
Leonard W. Hall, New York	1953–1957[a]	State legislator, 1927, 1928, 1934–1938; U.S. Representative, 1939–1952.
H. Meade Alcorn, Jr., Connecticut	1957–1959	State legislator, 1937–1941; Member of Republican National Committee, 1953–1961; Vice-Chairman of the Republican National Committee, 1956–1957.
Thruston B. Morton, Kentucky	1959–1961	U.S. Representative, 1947–1953; Assistant Secretary of State, 1953–1956; U.S. Senator, 1956–present.
William E. Miller, New York	1961–1964	U.S. Representative, 1950–1964; Chairman, National Republican Congressional Committee, 1960–1961.
Dean Burch, Arizona	1964–1965	Administrative Assistant to Senator Barry M. Goldwater, 1956–1959; Assistant Campaign Manager, Goldwater for President, 1963–1964.

Sources: *Who's Who in America; Biographical Directory of the American Congress,* 1774–1961.

[a] C. Wesley Roberts, Kansas, was National Chairman for a brief period in 1953.

strictly party matters for the President, and planning for future campaigns—presidential and congressional. When there is no Republican President, the Chairman functions more independently. He must
raise money and plan for campaigns, but he is called on more often
to speak for his party. As emphasized earlier, there is no single
clearly identifiable leader of the minority party, though there are any
number of alternatives—the titular leader, House and Senate minority leaders, former Presidents. The National Chairman is the only
man who presumably represents the extragovernmental party. Therefore, representatives of the news media will turn to him for comments
and statements, even on public policy questions. The Republicans
have not been notably successful in selecting chairmen who have been
able to gain press attention during the out years. In fact, the Chairman who received the most publicity in recent years has been Leonard W. Hall, National Chairman for four years during the Eisenhower
Administration.

Turnover has always been high among Republican National Chairmen. Table 2–1 shows that there have been 17 Chairmen since
1930 (compared to 12 for the Democrats during the same period).
No doubt this turnover is due in large part to the successive
defeats at the polls for Republicans. Table 2–1 also shows that
many Republican Chairmen since 1930 have had congressional
experience. As we noted before, Congress is a "retreat" for the minority party during those long periods when it is unable to capture the
White House. To the extent that there are leaders of the governmental party, they tend to be in Congress. It is interesting therefore
to see so many Congressmen and Senators selected as National
Chairmen. These men doubtless bring to the National Headquarters
the views of the congressional party.[13] Eight of the 17 Chairmen
since 1930 have had experience in Congress. Only 2 of the 12 Democratic National Chairmen during this period had congressional experience—Senators J. Howard McGrath and Henry M. Jackson. Prior to
1930, 8 of 27 Republican Chairmen and 7 of 18 Democratic Chairmen had congressional experience.[14] Thus there is some evidence to

[13] James MacGregor Burns, in his book *The Deadlock of Democracy: Four
Party Politics in America* (Englewood Cliffs, N.J.: Prentice-Hall, 1963),
makes a distinction between the congressional and presidential Republican
and Democratic parties—a distinction which is close to being a liberal-
conservative dichotomy. At one point, Burns argues that the Republican
congressional party proceeded to take over the Republican national machinery
in 1961 (see p. 284).

[14] Cotter and Hennessy provide statistics for all Republican and Democratic
National Chairmen, p. 65.

suggest that the minority party, whether it is Republican or Democratic, will tend to select National Chairmen from Congress more readily than will the majority party.

The National Committee[15]

Both parties elect members of their national committees in about the same way. All fifty states, the District of Columbia, Puerto Rico, and the Virgin Islands, are entitled to one committeeman and, since 1920 and women's suffrage, one committeewoman. These individuals are formally elected at the national convention but the nominating process is, in reality, the election process. Republican National Committee members are nominated by several different means: state primary in 4 states, state convention in 23 states, state central committee in 7 states, and by the delegates to the national convention in 16 states.[16] They serve four-year terms, from one national party convention to the next. Vacancies between conventions are filled by state party central committees.

Since 1952, certain Republican state party chairmen also serve on the National Committee. If Republican presidential electors were elected in the last presidential election, or the state has a Republican governor, or a majority of the state's congressional delegation is Republican, then that state's chairman serves on the National Committee. The Democrats do not follow this procedure. This enlargement of the Committee is specifically designed to overrepresent those states in which the Republican Party has had some measure of success. The Republican Party has always faced the problem of how to represent the hitherto moribund southern state Republican organizations at the convention and in the National Committee. As might be expected, southern Republicans fought the move to include state chairmen when the change was adopted at the 1952 Republican Convention.

The scheme of including state chairmen has had the effect of injecting more life into the National Committee, since (1) state party chairmen are more likely to be state party leaders than National Committee members, and (2) the Republican Party has been successful in recruiting an unusually able group of state chairmen (for example, Jean Tool, Colorado; Ray Bliss, Ohio; Judson Morhouse,

---

[15] See Cotter and Hennessy, in particular Ch. 2.
[16] See Cotter and Hennessy, pp. 30–31, for a map of which states use which system.

New York; Craig Truax, Pennsylvania; R. Mort Frayn, Washington; Robert Forsythe, Minnesota).

The Republican National Committee, like its Democratic counterpart, is more a collection than it is a group.[17] Several criteria are important in being selected, there is no consistent pattern state to state. Some are selected because of long service to the party—not necessarily in decision-making capacities. Others are major political figures in their states. Some are selected because of financial contributions made to the party or because they are friends of leading state politicians. All in all the Committee is diverse in background—too much so to act in a policy-making capacity. Further, it meets infrequently, one to three times a year. Little wonder that a 15-member Executive Committee is selected to serve in an advisory capacity to the Chairman.

The 15-member Executive Committee is elected by the National Committee at its first organizational meeting, which comes within fifteen days after the national convention. Careful attention is paid to represent geographical areas and committeewomen. This group is small enough so that the Chairman can call them together on rather short notice to handle any urgent problems or to get their approval of policy over the telephone.

In addition to the Chairman and the Executive Committee, there are several other officers of the National Committee. Four Vice-Chairmen, two men and two women, and a Secretary and Treasurer, are elected at the first organizational meeting of the National Committee. The Chairman then appoints a woman as Assistant Chairman (she also heads the women's division) and a General Counsel. All of these officers are ex officio members of the Executive Committee, as are the President of the National Federation of Republican Women and the Chairman of the Young Republican National Federation.

In theory, the National Committee has a great many tasks; Bone lists a total of thirteen.[18] But, as has been emphasized here, most of these are in fact exercised by the National Chairman, the National Headquarters, or some other unit designated to act for the National

[17] For details on who becomes a member of a national party committee, see Cotter and Hennessy, Ch. 3.

[18] Bone, pp. 118–125. The functions include: fund-raising, patronage, planning the national convention, symbolizing the party's national identity, criticizing, publicity and public relations, advertising party policy, custodian of the platform, maintaining party records, advising state and local organizations, collecting information on matters of party concern, testing strength of factions, and channeling communications between local party committeemen and their leaders.

Committee. There is, however, one task in which all committeemen and committeewomen actually get involved: preparation and general management of the quadrennial Republican National Convention. A number of committees and subcommittees are appointed—for example, a committee to select the convention city; a committee on arrangements with subcommittees on tickets; badges; concessions; decorations; convention program; housing; press, radio, and television; and transportation (see Table 3–2 Chapter 3). These committees and others are composed of members of the National Committee. The Committee on Arrangements, as with all such appointed committees, must, by party rule, have an equal number of men and women serving on it. It is composed of representatives from each state—either the committeeman or committeewoman.[19] It is the responsibility of each state's member to handle all administrative matters for his state delegation to the convention, though he will likely delegate some of the responsibility. The principal problems to deal with are guest ticket arrangements, housing arrangements, and distribution of convention patronage. Guest tickets are allocated to each state on the basis of the number of delegates to the National Convention, political performance of the Republican Party in the state, and distance from the convention city (those states nearby receive more tickets). All requests for tickets are directed to members of the National Committee in the state. Housing for a delegation is generally handled by a housing chairman responsible to the Committee member in charge of arrangements. Of course, as is true of all National Committee functions, the National Headquarters staff is very much involved in all the details of preparing for the National Convention.

A final chore for the state's representative on the Committee on Arrangements is to distribute convention patronage. Each state is allocated one Page, one Assistant Sergeant at Arms, and one Assistant Doorkeeper for every ten delegates or fraction thereof. There is no compensation for pages, but the Assistant Sergeants at Arms and doorkeepers receive a nominal payment if they actually perform the duties of the offices. Finally, there are appointments as honorary assistant sergeants at arms. These appointments carry neither official duties nor assignment of a seat in the Convention Hall. Those who hold these honorary positions can gain admittance to the Hall, but have to sit wherever they can find empty seats. They are commonly

---

[19] The host state always has all of its National Committee members on the Committee on Arrangements so that they can attend to local arrangements.

referred to as the "bird dogs" of the Convention–constantly seeking another place to sit.

In summary, the National Committee is the "capstone of the formal party organization," to use V. O. Key's description.[20] One should not expect, however, that a description of the formal organization will be an accurate description of the operating system. The Committee reflects the characteristics of Republican national party organization and therefore has diversified membership and little centralized authority.

Other National Party Units
The Republican National Finance Committee[21]

The fund-raising function of the National Committee is formally accomplished by a Finance Committee composed of the finance chairmen of the various state party central committees and other important representatives of states from which the campaign money usually comes. The chairman of the group is designated by the National Party Chairman. Much of the Republican fund-raising is centered in the Finance Committee and the group then distributes funds to the operating committees, that is, the National Committee, the National Republican Congressional Committee, the National Republican Senatorial Committee, and the Independent Television Committee (the latter established to coordinate both the use of television for campaigning and for fund-raising dinners, that is, closed-circuit arrangements). As might be expected when money is involved, there are frequent conflicts among the various recipient groups over amounts to be received.

In 1960 the Finance Committee sought to raise $7.8 million dollars. In fact they were able to exceed that figure. Their principal sources of funds were from large contributors (twelve prominent families contributed nearly $550,000 to the Republican party),[22]

---

[20] Key, p. 316.

[21] For a more detailed account of party finance, see Alexander Heard, *The Costs of Democracy* (Garden City, New York: Anchor Books, 1962); Herbert E. Alexander, *Money, Politics, and Public Reporting* (Princeton: Citizen's Research Foundation, 1960) and *Financing the 1960 Election* (Princeton: Citizen's Research Foundation, 1962); President's Commission on Campaign Costs, *Financing Presidential Campaigns* (Washington, D.C.: Government Printing Office, 1962); and Cotter and Hennessy, Ch. 9.

[22] Herbert E. Alexander, *Financing the 1960 Election* (Princeton: Citizen's Research Foundation, 1962), p. 61. The twelve families were duPont, Field, Ford, Harriman, Lehman, Mellon, Olin, Pew, Reynolds, Rockefeller, Vanderbilt, and Whitney. The duPonts and Rockefellers contributed over $250,000 of the total contributed by the twelve families.

dinners, state quotas, and business. It should be noted that the National Headquarters staff does much of the day-to-day administering of fund-raising drives.

National Republican Congressional and Senatorial Committees

Further evidence in support of the conclusion that the National Committee is atop a mound of individually autonomous units—most of which pay little heed to the Committee—can be found in the operations of the congressional campaign committees on Capitol Hill. Though the National Committee is nominally charged with the responsibility of coordinating the party's congressional campaign effort, the National Republican Congressional and Senatorial Committees exist to help Republicans get elected to Congress.

The House Committee is composed of one House member from each state having one or more Republican representatives. Members are elected biennially by their state congressional delegations, subject to approval by the Republican Conference—a meeting of all House Republicans (see Chapter 5). The committee elects from its members a Chairman, five Vice-Chairmen, a Secretary, a Treasurer, and an Executive Secretary. The Chairman then appoints an Executive Committee of five members. The Committee has its own staff.

The principal activities of the House Committee are research, field service, finance, and public relations. As is true with most Republican committees, the research work is excellent. District election data are collected and analyzed (especially on those districts which are marginal—that is, where the Republican candidate gained 45 to 55 per cent of the vote in the last election), precinct organization is studied, and a daily record is kept on Democratic incumbents—attendance, bills introduced, speeches made, voting record—which is then made available to the Republican challenger.

The public relations activities include press releases on Republican accomplishments in Congress, photographic services for Congressmen (for example, a Congressman may request photographs of himself and a group of constituents), technical aid for Congressmen in preparing radio and television appearances, assistance in preparing newsletters or press releases. The House Committee will also provide campaign literature and other aids for use in the constituency.

The Congressional Committee's field service is a rather recent innovation. Full-time fieldmen are available to assist congressional candidates. Most of the effort of fieldmen is in activating moribund local organizations and providing tips to inexperienced candidates.

Finally, the House Committee has the important function of distributing funds to congressional candidates. The money is allocated on the basis of need and possibility of success. Thus candidates in marginal districts receive more than those from safe districts or those who have no chance of victory whatsoever.

The Senate Committee is selected by the Senate Republican Conference—a meeting of all Senate Republicans—and the Chairman is appointed by the Chairman of the Conference. The Senate Committee staff is smaller than that of the House Committee, because although the functions of both committees are very much the same, there are many fewer potential candidates in any one congressional election (33 as compared with 435 in the House).

As with most party committees, there is little coordination between the congressional and senatorial committees and less between these committees and the National Committee. There is some exchange of research findings and occasionally staff of the three committees will meet for lunch to discuss their activities, but for the most part the various groups operate independently of one another. Hugh Bone reports that National Chairman Guy Gabrielson proposed in 1951 that there be consolidation of staff work of the Hill committees with the National Committee. The Hill committees vetoed the idea and even balked at Gabrielson's proposal for coordination meetings of the staffs.[23] Informal communication is the only means by which the efforts of these groups is coordinated.

Special Research and Advisory Groups

Following defeat at the polls, most political parties retire to examine the causes of defeat. The Republican Party has had many opportunities in the last thirty years to engage in this practice of self-analysis. Three such efforts deserve special treatment.[24]

After the crushing defeat in 1936, former President Herbert Hoover suggested that Republicans convene in a midterm convention to develop party positions. Though this idea was not implemented,

[23] Hugh A. Bone, *Party Committees and National Politics* (Seattle, Wash.: University of Washington Press, 1958), p. 151. Professor Bone has the only major work on these committees and this section has relied on his analysis. See in particular Ch. 5. See also "Some Notes on Congressional Campaign Committees," *Western Political Quarterly,* Vol. 9 (March, 1956), pp. 116–137.

[24] There was an earlier attempt to develop a party program in this century. In 1919–1920, a Republican Advisory Committee on Policies and Platforms, under the chairmanship of Will Hays, was formed. See Cotter and Hennessy, pp. 193–194, and all of Ch. 10.

the National Committee did establish a program committee of 100 Republican notables. Dr. Glenn Frank, former president of the University of Wisconsin, was appointed Chairman. The Frank Committee was soon enlarged to nearly 200 and was subdivided to work on policy problems. Though any effort on the part of an American political party to issue a statement of its policy positions is bound to have limited success, the Frank Committee did try valiantly and, after much squabbling, eventually issued a report in 1940. And, as Malcolm Moos notes, their formative meeting in 1938 is still the only effort on record of an American political party holding anything like a midterm convention to "structure party policy."[25]

In 1958, while General Eisenhower was still in the White House, congressional Republicans were defeated across the nation. Again the party decided to establish a national committee to study policy problems and issue a statement. National Chairman H. Meade Alcorn appointed 40 prominent Republicans to a Republican Committee on Program and Progress. The Chairman was Charles H. Percy, youthful president of Bell & Howell Company. The Committee was organized into four "task forces," each examining a general policy area: human rights and needs, the impact of science and technology, economic opportunity and progress, and national security and peace. After some seven months of deliberation, the Committee on Program and Progress issued its report entitled, *Decisions for a Better America.*[26] The report itself is a remarkable document—generally comprehensive and well written—but many Republicans complain that it has never been utilized as fully as they would like.

There was some effort to coordinate the work of the Committee on Program and Progress with the writing of the 1960 Republican platform. Percy was appointed Chairman of the Committee on Resolutions (the platform-writing committee) at the National Convention and Dr. Gabriel Hauge, chairman of one of the task forces, was Executive Secretary of the Committee on Resolutions. The 1960 platform was called *Building a Better America.*

After the 1960 election, National Chairman Thruston B. Morton appointed several committees to study the reasons for defeat. Three of the committees were directed to examine various electoral problems: insuring greater security and less fraud at polling places, increasing Republican voter registration, and improving state election laws. A

[25] Moos, p. 406.
[26] Republican Committee on Program and Progress, *Decisions for a Better America* (Garden City, N.Y.: Doubleday, 1960).

fourth committee was charged with the responsibility of examining big city politics, since it was obvious that in 1960 Republicans continued to lose by large margins in metropolitan areas. The "Committee on Big City Politics" was chaired by Ray Bliss, Republican State Chairman in Ohio. The Committee's report was extensive and made recommendations on party organization, candidate recruitment, interest group action, nationalities, minorities, public relations, and surveys. It was typical of all reports issued by the Republican National Committee in that the research was carefully done and the recommendations were sensible and to the point. Implementing the recommendations has proved difficult, however, for any number of reasons.[27]

State and Local Party Organization

There is an implicit assumption that American political parties are tightly and efficiently organized at the state and local level. This assumption follows from the oft-quoted statement that American political parties are decentralized. Since there are not powerful party hierarchies at the national level, it is implied that they exist at lower levels. It is a fact that the Republican Party does have relatively powerful party organization in some states (for example, Ohio, New York) but most state and local party organizations are more "paper" organizations than they are operating units. In the South, Republican Party organization has been nonexistent until recently. In many other states the organization is moribund between major state elections and becomes candidate-oriented during elections. In effect, state party organization is often no more than a list of persons with special skills, and/or inclinations, and/or access. These people can be activated to campaign for a candidate or slate of candidates but the organization again becomes just a list of names after election day. As the late V. O. Key, Jr., summarized it: "Often party is in a sense a fiction."[28]

[27] Chairman Morton discusses the post-1960 effort in an essay in Paul David, ed., *The Presidential Election and Transition* (Washington D.C.: The Brookings Institution, 1961). It should also be recorded that a recent group called the Republican Citizens Committee of the United States, chaired by President Eisenhower, has a "Critical Issues Council," which produced a number of papers during the 1964 preconvention period, no doubt designed to influence the platform writing at the convention. The "Council" was chaired by Dr. Milton Eisenhower.

[28] V. O. Key, Jr., *American State Politics* (New York: Knopf, 1956), p. 271.

Summary

Describing American parties is a difficult assignment. It is like trying to fit together a jigsaw puzzle by placing the pieces on rippling water. There is just no reason why the pieces should stay put; in fact, all forces work to destroy cohesion. So it is in describing Republican Party organization, with one additional qualification: the pieces weren't designed to fit together in the first place.

I have focused on the national party organization and emphasized that the day-to-day work at that level is done by a professional staff in the party Headquarters. The National Chairman sets general policy and symbolizes the national party organization more than does any other figure, particularly for the minority party. The National Committee has an impressive list of functions, but most of these are delegated to other party units.

Finally, I have tried to emphasize that the minority party national organization is constantly under pressure. It is presumably at the apex of an organization over which it really has minimal control. The national organization cannot accomplish what it is charged to accomplish; it simply lacks the authority. There is some doubt that it can even disband, for there is no one with enough power to kill the party. Yet, since it is the "only national organization we have," it is held responsible for defeats. To further compound the frustration of those who make up the Republican national organization, the accolades for victory usually go to the candidate—not to his staff.

CHAPTER **3**

Nominating Republicans

ANY POLITICAL SYSTEM must provide for some means of selecting leadership. In representative democracy, elections perform this function. Citizens choose from among their number certain able and knowledgeable individuals to act in their stead on public issues. In a complex society, this process of electing representatives becomes highly organized. Citizens do not vote for just anyone; they choose among those individuals who appear on a ballot. The process by which individuals get on the ballot is the central concern of this chapter.

I have stated that a principal function of American political parties is to organize elections. They recruit candidates, attempt to nominate party-endorsed candidates over other candidates, and make very effort to insure that their nominee wins public office on election day. Controlling nominations is the very life-blood of a political party. Yet, in the United States, efforts have been made to drain that life-blood from parties by attemping to take from them the power of controlling their own nominations. It is possible in this country to win the right to be the Republican candidate for many high offices by running in a primary election. Republican Party officials do not have the power to deny a candidate the nomination if he wins the primary. Many critics claim that ours is a weak, irresponsible party system which hinders rather than facilitates democratic government, yet few, if any, of these critics would recommend abolishing the direct primary. Indeed, some suggest extending it to presidential nominations.

The Direct Primary—The American Way of Nominating

The overwhelming majority of candidates for public office in America are nominated in primary elections. Presidential election years are particularly productive of primaries since there are both direct primaries, which are used to nominate state, local, and congressional candidates, and presidential primaries, which are used by some states to nominate delegates to the national conventions. In 1964, there were direct primaries in all 50 states—presidential primaries and/or preference polls in 16. Three states held direct primaries in April, 14 in May, 9 in June, 3 in July, 9 in August, 11 in September, and one in October. Presidential primaries were spread out over a four-month period. The first occurred, as always, in New Hampshire on March 10 and the last in California and South Dakota on June 2.

How is it that the direct primary became so popular? Before the turn of the century, most candidates were nominated in conventions called for that purpose. Delegates to nominating conventions were themselves selected by some local party group, usually a caucus or convention. Most conventions were dominated by strong party leaders who dictated their choices for public offices. Since America was at this time divided into one-party areas—that is, Democrats in the South and Republicans in the North and West—the fact that party leaders could select nominees meant that they were actually selecting public officials. The direct primary was developed to "break the hold of party oligarchies on the dominant party and to develop an intraparty politics."[1] The power to nominate candidates was taken from party leaders and given to the people. Instead of improving party organization, reformers sought to destroy it in favor of "direct democracy."

It is a maxim of American politics that no two states ever do anything alike. There are many variations of the direct primary. In Minnesota and Nebraska, state legislators are elected on a nonpartisan ballot and therefore the direct primaries for that office are nonpartisan, with the two candidates receiving the most votes appearing on the general election ballot. Other states have nonpartisan primaries for other offices. Partisan primaries are either "closed" or "open." Political parties prefer the "closed" primary, since voters are supposed to declare their party preference and vote only in that primary. Ten states maintain "open" primaries, however, where the voter is simply given a choice, in the secrecy of the polling booth, of which party primary he will participate in. He does not have to declare his party affiliation.

There are any number of modifications of the basic "closed-open" variation. In the South, Democrats rely on "runoff" primaries—a second primary if no candidate receives a majority in the first. California for many years allowed "cross-filing" whereby candidates from one party could file in the other party's primary and therefore win the nomination in both parties. Former Governor Earl Warren, a Republican, often won both the Republican and Democratic nominations for Governor. It is quite possible that many California Democrats still believe that Warren is a Democrat. He was their party's

[1] V. O. Key, Jr., *American State Politics* (New York: Knopf, 1956), p. 89.

candidate often enough. Other states have allowed variations of this technique. The state of Washington employs the so-called "blanket primary" whereby the voter receives a ballot with both parties' candidates listed and can actually split his primary vote between the two parties.

Parties have reacted to these "antiparty" techniques by trying to control the direct primary. Informal efforts are made to insure that the party will have only one strong candidate in the primary. When party leaders are recruiting candidates, they may guarantee that their choice will not have opposition in the primary. Indeed, a leading member of the community may agree to run on the condition that party leaders persuade all other possible contenders to withdraw from the primary. Parties have been quite successful in employing these informal techniques of persuasion to avoid the intraparty feuds that can so easily develop as a result of bitter primary elections.

A more formal mechanism for making the direct primary a party-oriented event is the "preprimary" convention. In these meetings, the party endorses a single candidate for an office, so that there is an official party slate in the primary. In some states, principally those where there is strong party organization to begin with, this has been an effective device for insuring party control of candidacies. There is risk involved in this device, however. What if other candidates, not endorsed at the convention, refuse to be intimidated and not only run but win, without party endorsement? Meeting in a preprimary convention in 1956, Wisconsin Republicans endorsed Congressman Glenn Davis for the Senate seat then held by Senator Alexander Wiley. Senator Wiley did not withdraw and defeated Davis handily in the primary. Wiley was able to demonstrate his personal strength in a contest with his own party organization. The Wisconsin Republican Party organization did not soon recover from this humiliation.

The late V. O. Key, Jr., provided us with more data on primaries than has any other student of political parties. Several of his findings are of direct significance to the Republican Party. In general it is true that the safer the seat, the more likely it is that there will be competition within the stronger party's primary. Key presents convincing evidence to support his point in his examination of Democratic gubernatorial races.[2] The strong Democratic states are characterized by primaries wherein the victorious candidate has vigorous opposition. The weak Democratic states are characterized by primaries wherein

[2] Key, Ch. 2.

the victorious candidate has little or no opposition. There is some difficulty in applying this proposition to the Republican Party. As has been indicated, there simply are fewer strong Republican states —and none which are as Republican in state and local elections as certain southern states are Democratic. In many southern states there are not even any Republican candidates in the general election. Furthermore, the tendency is clearly in the direction of greater competition in states where the Republican candidate is more likely to win in the general election.

Because of (1) the tendency for greater primary competition in the stronger Republican states and (2) the fact that the strongest Republican states are considerably more competitive in general elections than are the strongest Democratic states, hotly contested primaries have sometimes resulted in Republican defeats in the general elections. For example, in a state like Maine, traditionally a strong Republican state, the Democrats are able to garner a respectable percentage of the vote even in defeat. Republicans in Georgia, until recently, have not been so fortunate. Thus, when there is a divisive primary battle in Maine, it is possible for the Democrats to win in November. When there is a bitter divisive primary in Georgia, the Democrats still win in November because of their overwhelming dominance in the state.[3] I recently asked a prominent Maine Republican why the party was so successful in 1960 (winning the governorship, three House seats, and reelecting Senator Margaret Chase Smith) after a series of recent setbacks. He replied that is was the first time in several years that the party was able to avoid divisive primary battles.

Nominating a Presidential Candidate—The Republican Version

In his monograph "The Condition of Our National Political Parties," Stephen K. Bailey suggests that "the shortest route through the maze of national party structure begins with the presidential nominating conventions."[4] Thus, if one really wants to see the Republican Party, he should attend the National Convention. The party will be there—its leaders, its rank and file, its riffraff. The Convention is the perfect place for the observer to capture the disunity, disorganization, and lack of singularity of purpose of the national Republican Party.

[3] With the growth of Republican organization in the South, divisive Democratic primaries may in the future be more costly to the Democrats.
[4] (New York: Fund for the Republic, 1959), p. 7.

Of course, there are a few people at every National Convention who understand the life of such an operation. They usually win something there. The great majority of convention-goers do not understand the "grand design," however, and simply wander around for a week, proving yet again that any meeting of more than five people cannot make policy.

The Pre-Convention Campaign

National nominating conventions do not just happen. I have already alluded to the role played by the National Committee in the detailed preparation necessary for a National Convention. There also are many other forms of activity before the Convention. Most importantly, delegates must be selected and candidates who wish to be considered for nomination must garner delegate support. Increasingly, the party's choice for presidential candidates is obvious either because the party has an incumbent President as leader or because one man is successful in winning the pre-convention campaign. William G. Carleton argues that the candidate will be selected by the instruments of mass democracy; thus the National Convention is left to ratify the popular choice for the nomination. I would not argue that the obvious choice is necessarily the popular choice, but rather that he will become the candidate because he already leads the party or is successful in the pre-convention maneuvering. The nominating convention that actually makes a choice among candidates will be as rare in the future as it has been in the past.[5]

Election of Delegates. Nearly one half of National Convention delegates are selected by presidential primaries. There are two main purposes of presidential primaries: to select Convention delegates and to test the strength of presidential contenders. Both purposes may be combined in the presidential primary—that is, a slate of delegates preferring one candidate over another may be elected and therefore will likely vote for that man at the convention. The second purpose, testing strength of contenders, is accomplished

[5] See William G. Carleton, "The Revolution in the Presidential Nominating Convention," *Political Science Quarterly,* Vol. 72 (June, 1957), pp. 224–237. See also Nelson W. Polsby and Aaron Wildavsky, *Presidential Elections: Strategies of American Electoral Politics* (New York: Scribner, 1964), Ch. 4. Polsby and Wildavsky are critical of the Carleton thesis that the candidate is determined by popular choice before the National Convention. My position is that increasingly the candidate becomes obvious before the Convention. He may well not be the popular choice; for example, Goldwater in 1964.

by the presidential preference poll, appended to the primary in some states.

Wisconsin introduced the presidential primary to the American political scene in 1908 (the law was passed in 1905). By 1916, at least 22 states had such laws and several other states had flirted with the idea. Since that time, the number with primary laws has fluctuated from 16 to 19. Though several states have abandoned the device since the period of "primary fever," 1908 to 1916, none have adopted it.

Paul David and his colleagues, in their book *The Politics of National Party Conventions,* classify presidential primaries into four types, depending on whether and how delegates indicate their preference among candidates.[6]

Type I—The ballot does not show the delegate's preference among presidential contenders. In these states, the presidential primary is usually coupled with a preference poll which indicates voters' preference among contenders. (D/C, Ill., Neb., Pa., W. Va.)

Type II—The ballot may show the convention delegate's preference among presidential contenders if the contender consents. Delegates may also run on a "no-preference" basis. (Mass., N.J., S.D.)

Type III—The ballot may show the delegate's preference among presidential contenders, whether or not the contender consents. Delegates may also run on a "no-preference" basis. (Fla., N.H., Ore.)

Type IV—The ballot must show the delegate's preference among presidential contenders. (Calif., Ohio, Wisc.)

Presidential preference polls are of two types: advisory and mandatory. In the advisory poll, those presidential contenders who enter are running a "horse race" that may result in no delegate votes at all. That is, the two events—the primary and the poll—can be quite unrelated. Voters elect Convention delegates in the primary and vote their preference among those presidential contenders who have entered their names in the poll. There is the possibility that delegates will be elected who are committed to a different man from the one who wins the preference poll. For example, in 1960, Kennedy won the preference poll in West Virginia, but the delegates who were elected were reportedly committed to either Senator Stuart Symington or Senator Lyndon B. Johnson.[7]

---

[6] Paul David, *et. al., The Politics of National Party Conventions* (Washington D.C.: The Brookings Institution, 1960), Ch. 10.

[7] By ballot time at the Convention, however, Kennedy was able to garner 15 of the 25 delegate votes from West Virginia.

Mandatory preference polls bind the delegates to vote for the presidential contender who wins the poll. Oregon's law is the most interesting of the three states that still have mandatory polls. The Secretary of State in Oregon has absolute discretion to place on the ballot all contenders for President and Vice-President who are generally recognized as being candidates. Their consent is not required, though a man may withdraw his name by signing an affidavit that he is not a candidate (as Governor George Romney, Michigan, did in 1964). Delegates are bound to vote for the winner on the first two ballots, unless the candidate receives less than 35 per cent of the Convention vote.

Delegates not elected in primaries are selected by state or district party conventions or by a state party committee. There are too many variations of procedure to discuss here. Some of these delegates are given express mandates to vote for a particular presidential contender, or they are given no mandate, or possibly they are given a mandate of "noncommitment"—that is, to go to the National Convention uninstructed.

Pre-Convention Campaigning by Contenders. As is clearly illustrated by Paul David and his coauthors, the nature of pre-convention campaigning or the Convention itself depends upon whether the party is confirming existing leadership or is in the process of selecting new leadership. If it is confirming present leadership—either renominating a President (for example, Eisenhower, 1956) or nominating a Vice-President who succeeded to the Presidency (for example, Coolidge, 1924)—the pre-convention and Convention phases are rather cut-and-dried affairs. The same is true if the party has an obvious choice in selecting new leadership (for example, Nixon, 1960). There are usually more Conventions which confirm leadership or select the obvious man than otherwise (10 of the 17 in this century can be so classified). Every so often, however, the party finds itself without an obvious choice before the pre-convention campaign. When this happens the pre-convention and/or Convention phases become critical in determining who the candidate will be.[8] Selecting new party leadership is never a very pleasant or tidy business. For example, the Republican Party in this century has had at least five explosive nominating conventions: in 1912, 1920, 1940, 1952, and 1964. All

---

[8] A good discussion of the "strategic environment" of pre-convention campaigning may be found in Nelson W. Polsby and Aaron Wildavsky, *Presidential Elections: Strategies of American Electoral Politics* (New York: Scribner, 1964), Ch. 1.

five conventions were characterized by pre-convention periods wherein there were party leadership struggles.

In recent years the pre-convention campaign has become a much more public activity. Presidential contenders set out to prove that they are the popular choice and should receive the nomination. Presidential primaries have been important in this regard. As Paul David and his coauthors note: "In some respects the primaries may be said to have come into their own for the first time in the Republican campaign of 1952 . . ."[9] Though there are no studies of the extent to which there have actually been contests between contenders (or their delegates) in presidential primaries throughout the nation, one needs only to recall various conventions before 1952 to conclude that it has only recently been used as a device by candidates for parlaying their popularity into a presidential nomination. Harold Stassen, Estes Kefauver, Dwight D. Eisenhower, John F. Kennedy, popularized the presidential primary.

In 1952, many important Republican leaders were dissatisfied with the prospect of having "Mr. Republican," Senator Robert A. Taft, as their nominee in a year in which the party seemed to have an excellent chance of winning the White House. One of these Republican leaders was Governor Thomas E. Dewey of New York. Dewey, along with Senator Henry Cabot Lodge from Massachusetts and others, persuaded General Eisenhower, then Commanding General of the Allied Powers in Europe, to seek the nomination. Eisenhower agreed to have his name entered in the New Hampshire presidential primary. Though he never campaigned in New Hampshire—indeed he never left Paris—Eisenhower won by over 10,000 votes. The test in New Hampshire having been won, Eisenhower's strategists proceeded on a campaign to show his great vote-drawing ability. Their immediate interest was less in winning delegates in presidential primaries than in demonstrating to party leaders throughout the country why the party should select the popular war hero.

Following the New Hampshire victory, from which Taft could never fully recover because the Eisenhower strategists had made their point hard and early, Eisenhower received over 100,000 write-in votes in the Minnesota primary (losing to favorite son Harold Stassen by 20,000 votes; Taft did not enter) won impressive victories in New Jersey, Massachusetts, Pennsylvania, and Oregon. Taft won in Nebraska, Illinois, and West Virginia, states which Eisen-

---

[9] David, *et al.,* p. 278.

hower did not enter. Once again, the point was made and hammered home. In their last direct encounter, Eisenhower lost to Taft in South Dakota by only 816 votes out of a total vote of nearly 130,000. Taft had campaigned in South Dakota for five days. Eisenhower made no personal appearances at all; in fact, his name did not even appear on the ballot. Eisenhower delegates were entered as "no preference" delegates and thus the Eisenhower boosters had to conduct a campaign to educate the voters to this fact.

Meanwhile, George Gallup's polls were substantiating what was being said by Dewey and Lodge. Less than three weeks before the opening of the Republican National Convention, the Gallup Poll showed that Eisenhower was favored to defeat either Governor Adlai E. Stevenson or Senator Estes Kefauver, the Democratic frontrunners, by wide margins. The same poll showed Taft trailing the two Democrats.

This focus on Eisenhower in 1952 should not detract from Taft's efforts. Taft, too, was intent upon proving that he could win, and his pre-convention campaign organization was probably the largest and most active of any to that date.

In 1956, both parties confirmed leadership; the Republicans renominated their popular President and the Democrats renominated Adlai E. Stevenson. In 1960, Senator John F. Kennedy adopted the strategy of winning the Democratic nomination through demonstrating his popular appeal. He made the "art of the primary," as Theodore White refers to it, a fine art.[10] Richard M. Nixon, though the obvious choice for Republicans, still entered several primaries in order to demonstrate conclusively that he was the obvious choice for Republicans.

In 1964, the Republicans once again found themselves in a situation where there was no obvious nominee prior to pre-convention campaigning. Nixon had lost by the narrowest of margins in 1960 and seemed the logical choice for the nomination in 1964. In 1962, however, Nixon was defeated by an impressive margin in his effort to become Governor of California. He took himself out of the race after his defeat. Governor Nelson A. Rockefeller seemed the most logical choice after his reelection in 1962, but his personal life, particularly his remarriage, became a political liability. Senator Barry M. Goldwater assumed the "most obvious choice" label for some months, but

[10] Theodore White, *The Making of the President, 1960* (New York: Atheneum, 1961), Ch. 4.

President Kennedy's assassination dealt a severe blow to his chances. Goldwater's strategy was to combine a southern revolt with mid-western and western support to defeat the young President. When Vice-President Johnson succeeded to the Presidency, the Goldwater strategy seemed less promising, since Johnson was popular in the South and West. Thus, the pre-convention campaign period was as critical in 1964 for the Republicans as it had been in 1960 for the Democrats. And both of the leading contenders, Rockefeller and Goldwater, campaigned vigorously to demonstrate their popularity. Neither had much success.

The early primaries substantiated that there was no obvious choice. Henry Cabot Lodge, then Ambassador to South Viet Nam, won the New Hampshire primary on March 10. Goldwater was second in the preference poll and Rockefeller a close third. During April, the primary results were ambiguous. Congressman John Byrnes won the Wisconsin primary on April 7 as a favorite son. Neither Rockefeller nor Goldwater entered. Goldwater won the Illinois advisory preference poll on April 14. His opponent was Senator Margaret Chase Smith. No presidential candidates entered the New Jersey primary on April 21, though Lodge led in scattered write-in votes. On April 28, Lodge won the Massachusetts advisory preference poll and Governor William W. Scranton the Pennsylvania advisory preference poll, both with write-in votes.

By May, Lodge, Goldwater, Scranton, and Byrnes had won something. On May 5, Goldwater won the Indiana mandatory preference poll against perennial candidate Harold Stassen, and Governor James Rhodes won Ohio's primary as a favorite son. Goldwater won the Nebraska advisory preference poll on May 12, though Nixon garnered an impressive write-in vote, and Rockefeller won the West Virginia advisory preference poll on the same day without opposition. Rockefeller's long campaign effort began to reap benefits on May 15 when he won the Oregon mandatory preference poll against the field of candidates. None of the contenders was entered in the Maryland primary, May 19, and an uncommitted, pro-Goldwater slate of delegates won over a committed, pro-Goldwater slate in Florida on May 26.

The stage was set for the last two primaries, both occurring on June 2. The South Dakota primary was a contest between two slates of delegates—a formal Goldwater slate and a "no preference" slate with several pro-Goldwater delegates as members. The "no preference" slate won. In California, the two announced candidates, Goldwater and Rockefeller, entered the championship round. No other candidates were entered and write-ins were not possible. The two candidates had both spent a great deal of campaign time, effort, and money, in California. The Goldwater slate of delegates won by a narrow margin, 60,000 votes out of over 2 million votes cast. After months of campaigning, an obvious choice began to emerge.

A review of Senator Goldwater's strategy suggests that he was not content to rely on his popular appeal for winning the nomination. Between 1960 and 1964, Goldwater made hundreds of fund-raising speeches for the Republican Party at national, state, and local levels. He seldom declined an invitation to speak. He was an attractive figure and drew large audiences. His supporters worked hard to organize the party for Goldwater in areas where party organization was weak or nonexistent. Thus, in those states where National Convention delegates are selected by state conventions and state central committees, and therefore where party officials are important in delegate selection, Senator Goldwater was able to have his people designated as delegates. The vast majority of those delegates committed to him before the convention were selected by means other than the primary. On the first ballot, he won 292 of 303 delegate votes from southern states (including Kentucky). Of these southern delegates, only those in Florida were selected by presidential primary; the rest were selected by state and district conventions and state party committees. Of the states west of the Mississippi River (excluding Texas), Goldwater garnered 329 out of 390 votes. Of these states, only California and Oregon have presidential primaries. Goldwater won the important California primary and lost the Oregon primary to Rockefeller. The Arizona Senator had nearly enough votes (621) from the South and West to win on the first ballot. He was then able to go to other state party leaders, for example, those in Illinois and Ohio, and present them with the certainty of his nomination. Though the polls showed him trailing Governor Scranton among those voters who identify with the Republican Party, and his performance in the primaries had been unimpressive, he could remain confident that his strategy had given him delegate support.

Goldwater complemented his strategy of picking up delegate strength through state and district conventions by judicious use of presidential primaries. Though he entered several other primaries where he would have only token opposition, the New Hampshire, Oregon, and California primaries were initially selected for serious campaigning. Following Ambassador Lodge's victory in New Hampshire, however, Goldwater and his staff decided against campaigning in Oregon, where there were so many "phantom" opponents, as he called them. Thus, the California primary became the capstone of the pre-convention campaign. Goldwater had collected an impressive total of delegates by June 2, far more than had any other candidate. The California victory proved that he could win against strong opposition and, more importantly at that point, he added 86 delegate votes to his total. Immediately following the electronic computer's declaration that Goldwater would win in California, which came just twenty-two minutes after most polls had closed, commentators spoke of Goldwater's victory on the first ballot at the convention.

The post-California primary atmosphere was almost eerie. The eastern, moderate wing of the party, which had dominated national party conventions in recent years, realized that Senator Goldwater would be the nominee unless action were taken. The Annual Governors' Conference in Cleveland in early June was the center of efforts to launch a counteroffensive to Goldwater. Many Republican governors were dissatisfied with a Goldwater candidacy, but they could agree on no one to lead an anti-Goldwater drive, nor were they assured of victory if they tried.

Following the Governors' Conference, Governor Scranton announced his intention to seek the nomination. Lodge's supporters backed Scranton's bid, and Rockefeller withdrew from the race in favor of Scranton. Though the odds were heavily against him, Scranton immediately began a nationwide tour to contact unpledged delegates and to convince Goldwater delegates to switch allegiances. He appealed to delegates and party leaders to consider the probable losses on state and local tickets if Goldwater were the nominee.

Meanwhile, other moderate Republicans began to concentrate on the platform. If they could not have a candidate of their choosing, then they wanted to force Senator Goldwater to moderate his views by forcing him to accept a platform that was moderate, rather than conservative, in tone. All such efforts by the moderates were doomed to fail. Senator Goldwater and his strategists had locked up the nomination before the convention and they were not in a conciliatory mood.

Despite the fact that its boundaries are rather ill-defined, it has become quite apparent that the pre-convention campaign is of increasing importance in the process of nominating a presidential candidate. If the party has no obvious choice, then the choice will probably become obvious during the months before the convention. If the party does have an incumbent leader, then that man will likely enter presidential primaries to demonstrate his vote-getting ability. In recent years, the presidential primary has become an important tool for presidential contenders in their attempt to prove to the party that they can win. The 1964 Republican pre-convention campaign will no doubt always stand as an exception to this generalization. Of course, it may well be that no candidate is able to prove his popularity in the pre-convention period or collect a majority of delegates by other means—that all candidates trying to do so are defeated by one another. This being the case, the National Convention will make the choice, the party will be divided, and a Democrat will probably be elected President.

The Republican National Convention

With the pre-convention campaigning over, the delegates selected, the National Committee's plans completed, and the last red, white, and blue banner stapled in place, Republicans are ready to attempt to demonstrate that a crowd can make a rational decision. Thousands of loyal members of the Grand Old Party file into one of America's large cities, most often Chicago (See Table 3–2), in the heat of the summer for the major purpose of selecting a presidential candidate. For those who do not understand America and her politics, the Convention must seem both strange and not a little uncouth. For those who do understand and love American politics, it all seems rather grand.

The Delegates

There is a definite formula for apportioning delegates among the several states that is adopted at each Convention to serve as the basis for membership at the next Convention. In 1960, the Committee on Rules of the National Convention adopted the following formula for 1964 (which resulted in a total of 1,308 delegates at the 1964 Convention).[11]

A. Delegates at Large

1. Four Delegates at Large from each State.

2. Two additional Delegates at Large for each Representative at Large in Congress from each State.

3. Nine Delegates at Large for District of Columbia, five Delegates

[11] Taken from the Rules of the 1960 Republican National Convention.

at Large for Puerto Rico and three Delegates at Large for the Virgin Islands.

4. Six additional Delegates at Large from each State casting its electoral vote, or a majority thereof, for the Republican nominee for President in the last preceding Presidential election. If any State does not cast its electoral vote or a majority thereof for the Republican nominee in the last preceding Presidential election, but at that election or at a subsequent election held prior to the next Republican National Convention elects a Republican United States Senator or a Republican Governor then in such event such State shall be entitled to such additional Delegates at Large.

B. District Delegates

1. One District Delegate from each Congressional District casting two thousand (2,000) votes or more for the Republican nominee for President or for any elector pledged to vote for the Republican nominee for President in the last preceding Presidential election, or for the Republican nominee for Congress in the last preceding Congressional election.

2. One additional District Delegate for each Congressional District casting ten thousand (10,000) votes or more for the Republican nominee for President or for any elector pledged to vote for the Republican nominee for President in the last preceding Presidential election, or for the Republican nominee for Congress in the last preceding Congressional election.

C. Alternate Delegates

One Alternate Delegate to each Delegate to the National Convention.

Who are the delegates? Paul David and his colleagues have provided an extensive compilation of delegate characteristics.[12] In general, Republican delegates tend to be white, Protestant, well-educated men of considerable means and in prestige occupations (lawyers, businessmen, and professional men). There is an increasing number of women delegates, but they are still in the vast minority. About 40 per cent of Republican delegates will have been to prior conventions, so turnover is rather high (a result, no doubt, of the fact that one reason for selecting a delegate is to reward party service). The delegation probably contains important party leaders in the state, though this is not always the case.[13]

There are any number of criteria which may be used for selecting

[12] David, *et. al.,* Ch. 14. See also Paul Tillett, ed., *Inside Politics: The National Conventions, 1960* (Dobbs Ferry, N.Y.: Oceana, 1962), pp. 131–144.

[13] For example, in 1960, the South Dakota delegation was essentially a leaderless delegation, almost by design. See Tillett (ed.), pp. 160–170.

the delegates or in preparing a slate for a primary or a state convention. For example, in 1960, the South Dakota Republican State Central Committee, along with the national committeeman and committeewoman, rewarded party service, tried to represent geographical sections and economic interests of the state, honored requests of party leaders, and continued to exclude the congressional delegation, since they would attend anyway as guests of the National Convention.[14]

Planning the Convention[15]

As previously noted, the National Committee and its Headquarters have the principal responsibility for planning the National Convention. A first order of business is selecting the site. The National Chairman appoints a Site Selection Committee to assist him in this important decision. In 1963, the Site Selection Committee was composed of six members: three national committeemen and three national committeewomen. Mr. Jean Tool, Colorado State Republican Chairman, served as Chairman. There are many considerations in selecting a city for the Convention: it must have a large, air-conditioned hall; a great many hotel rooms; adequate transportation facilities; facilities for the mass media, particularly television; and the city selected must be willing to contribute a great deal of money toward Convention expenses. In late summer, 1963, the Republican Site Selection Committee reviewed seven cities: Atlantic City, Chicago, Dallas, Detroit, Miami Beach, Philadelphia, and San Francisco. San Francisco was chosen, since it agreed to pay $650,000 toward Convention expenses, was willing to provide free office space, meeting rooms, and accommodations for Convention officials, and Republicans had been well satisfied with their treatment in that city in 1956. A city is willing to contribute money and provide accomodations because a national convention brings with it a great deal of publicity for the city and literally millions of dollars (an estimated $6 million for San Francisco in 1964) for the hotels, merchants, night clubs, restaurants, and transportation facilities.

Other planning committees appointed by the Chairman are the

[14] Tillett (ed.), p. 160.
[15] The Arts and Sciences Division of the Republican National Committee, under the leadership of Dr. John Kessel, published an excellent survey of how the Republican Party plans a convention in its February, 1964, issue of *Republican Report*. This survey has been valuable in preparing this section of the book.

Committee on Call, the Committee on Rules, the Committee on Contests, and the Committee on Arrangements. The latter committee is in charge of all physical arrangements and has already been discussed. (See Chapter II.) It does its work through various subcommittees (housing, tickets, transportation, badges, etc.). The Committee on Call is responsible for setting the date and time of the Convention, verifying the number of delegates allocated to each state, according to the formula established in the previous Convention, and, after the Call has been approved by the National Committee, sending four copies of the Call to each state central committee.

The Committee on Rules reviews the rules and recommends any changes deemed necessary. In 1964 the Committee considered the rules for the 1968 Convention, rule changes for the 1964 Convention, and procedures for National Committee operations between 1964 and 1968. All rule changes must be ultimately approved by the Convention Committee on Rules and Order of Business (see below) and by the Convention itself.

The Committee on Contests is a small, fact-finding agency for the National Committee. All credentials for delegates and alternates must be filed with the Secretary of the National Committee at least twenty-five days before the Convention meets. If there are disputes, the Committee on Contests issues a statement that sets forth the rules governing the election of delegates from the state and the contentions of the disputants. The Committee on Contests then makes a judgment on the dispute and reports it to the National Committee. A temporary roll of delegates is then prepared by the Secretary of the National Committee. Further disputes over legitimate delegates are resolved by the Convention Committee on Credentials (see below), which has the responsibility of preparing the permanent roll of delegates.

In addition to the planning done by these committees, the National Headquarters staff is preoccupied with convention arrangements for about a year before the convention. A great deal of paper work, research, and telephoning is necessary so that the planning committees themselves can perform their functions. In addition, there is the problem of insuring that newspapers, radio, and television are properly accommodated at the convention city.

Convention Organization

Despite all appearances, there *is* organization at a national convention. Though this organization may seem unconventional, it can be explained very simply. Recall that the National Committee has been designated to act for the party between Conventions. When Republicans meet in National Convention, that body once again assumes its supreme position as principal decision-maker for the party. The mandate of the National Committee ceases when the Convention convenes. Thus, the problem is that of the Committee's closing out its functions and facilitating a transfer of functions to the Convention.

The technique for facilitating the transfer of functions to the Convention is that of having a temporary organization. Particularly important are the four standing committees, which should not be confused with planning committees of the Republican National Committee (see Table 3–1). The Committee on Credentials examines the credentials of delegates, hears challenges to the right of delegates to be seated at the Convention, and prepares a permanent roll of delegates. The Committee on Rules and Order of Business considers the rules to govern the conduct of the Convention. The Committee on Permanent Organization compiles a list of permanent convention officials and recommends this list for adoption by the convention. Normally, the more important positions have already been suggested by the National Committee. Any controversy that develops over who will be the Permanent Chairman is resolved before the Permanent Organization Committee meets. Finally, the Committee on Resolutions has the unenviable task of drafting the platform for presentation to the Convention. The first three committees above are composed of one person from each state delegation. The Committee on Resolutions is composed of two representatives from each delegation—a man and a woman.

There is seldom any controversy over the work of the Committees on Credentials, Rules and Order of Business, and Permanent Organization. They meet, accomplish their functions with dispatch, and present their conclusions to the National Convention for approval. Of these three, only the Committee on Credentials ever has much difficulty and on at least two occasions in this century, their work has been the focus of attention owing to contested delegations. In 1912, there were important contests between delegates pledged to President William Howard Taft and those pledged to former President Theodore Roosevelt. For the most part, the Taft delegates won the right to be seated.

In 1952, the seating of delegates became a major issue between the backers of Robert A. Taft and Dwight D. Eisenhower. The prob-

Table 3–1. Planning Committees for a Republican National Convention

Committees and Subcommittees of the Republican National Committee and Their Function	*Temporary Committees of the Republican National Convention and Their Function*
Site Selection Committee — selects site of convention.	Committee on Credentials — examines credentials of delegates, reviews disputes, prepares permanent roll.
Committee on Arrangements — in charge of all physical arrangements.	Committee on Rules and Order of Business — recommends rules to Convention.
Subcommittees: Tickets; Badges; Concessions; Decorations; Convention Program; Housing; Press, Radio, Television; Transportation.	Committee on Permanent Organization — compiles list of permanent convention officials.
Committee on Call — sets the date of the Convention, verifies allocation of delegates, issues the Call.	Committee on Resolutions — prepares platform for Convention.
Committee on Rules — reviews rules, recommends changes.	
Committee on Contests — reviews disputes over delegations, compiles temporary roll.	

Sources: *Republican Report,* Arts and Sciences Division, Republican National Committee, Vol. III (February, 1964), and "1964 GOP Convention Fact Sheet," Republican National Committee, June 16, 1964.

lem centered on seating delegates from Georgia, Louisiana, and Texas. Both the Taft and Eisenhower forces had manuevered to control the southern delegations. There was evidence that in Louisiana the Taft forces, who had more access to state party leadership than the Eisenhower forces, were running roughshod over Eisenhower majorities in party meetings.[16] Eisenhower's backers came to the Convention complaining about "steals," "The Great Texas Swindle," "ruthless tactics of the Old Guard," "Taft machine politics." The National

[16] The Eisenhower forces published a document called "The Louisiana Story," which provided their version of the details involved in electing delegates in that state. A similar document on Texas was entitled "The Great Texas Swindle."

Committee heard arguments on both sides before the Convention and, for purposes of establishing the temporary roll, allowed all of the Taft delegates from Georgia, most of those from Louisiana, and accepted Taft's compromise for Texas.

The Committee on Credentials of the National Convention was the second arena of debate. For two stormy days, the contending forces argued their case before the Committee on Credentials and the television cameras. The Committee then voted to seat the Taft delegates from Georgia, to seat the Eisenhower delegates from Louisiana after a Taft capitulation, and, by a very narrow margin, to accept Taft's formula for Texas (22 Taft delegates and 16 Eisenhower delegates). Taft's surrender of his Louisiana delegates was intended as a peace overture to prevent the credentials battle from going to the floor of the convention. But the Eisenhower backers had their issue and they continued to press it.

Eisenhower's supporters were able to get a reading on the mood of the Convention on opening day. The Annual Governors' Conference was held just before the Republican Convention and in that meeting 23 of 25 of the Republican governors signed a manifesto urging that contested delegates not be allowed to vote in the Convention until after all contests were settled. This suggestion was introduced as a "fair play" amendment to the rules on Monday, July 7, 1952. After acrimonious debate, the amendment passed unanimously, following a roll-call vote on a modifying amendment offered by a Taft supporter, Congressman Clarence Brown from Ohio. Brown's pro-Taft amendment to the amendment was defeated, 658 to 548. This vote was the first real test between Eisenhower and Taft.

Both a majority and minority report were presented to the National Convention by the Committee on Credentials. In an emotion-charged atmosphere, the Convention accepted the minority report on Georgia and therefore seated the pro-Eisenhower delegates. A Taft delegate then made the motion to accept the minority report on Texas so as to avoid another roll-call defeat. Thus Eisenhower delegates from all three states were seated and, according to most observers, the Convention was all but over.[17]

The Committee on Resolutions, or Platform Committee, has an important task to perform and begins its work a week or more before

17 For further details on this contest see, Paul David, *et al.,* pp. 262–263, 556–559; Malcolm Moos, *The Republicans, A History of Their Party* (New York: Random House, 1956), pp. 470–479; and Dwight D. Eisenhower, *Mandate for Change* (Garden City, N.Y.: Doubleday, 1963), pp. 42–43.

the Convention. The Committee hears testimony from interest groups and others who wish to express their views. In 1960, most of the work of hammering out the details of the platform was done by eight subcommittees. In 1964, a thirteen-man subcommittee was appointed to write an initial draft of the platform and the Committee on Resolutions worked as a whole. There is always some controversy involved in constructing a broad party statement, even though most delegates realize that the platform does not have a very significant function in American politics. It is the case that the members of the Platform Committee are often the more serious, hard-working delegates. They come early to the Convention city and have to work long hours in order to develop a document which in general represents the party's views on major issues. Various presidential aspirants will try to have their supporters placed in important positions on the Platform Committee, but all in all, it is not easy for contenders to control the process by which each state selects its Platform Committee members.

Controversy developed in 1960 over the writing of the platform. Late in the week before the Convention, it became apparent that some of the subcommittees of the Platform Committee were preparing planks which neither followed closely the Percy Report, *Decisions for a Better America* (see Chapter 2), nor were in line with Vice President Nixon's views. This was particularly true for the civil rights plank. Southern members of the Civil Rights Subcommittee were pressing for a relatively weak plank, whereas Nixon preferred an extensive civil rights statement. While the Subcommittee was working on its draft, the Vice-President met with Governor Nelson A. Rockefeller to iron out any disagreements between them over the platform. The result of this meeting was a statement intended to act as a guideline for the Platform Committee. Many delegates criticized the statement as being "dictatorial," and proceeded to ignore Nixon's wishes. The Civil Rights Subcommittee rejected the Nixon-Rockefeller version in favor of a southern version. The full Committee also adopted the southern version. The Vice-President arrived in Chicago on Monday and immediately began to press for reconsideration of the civil rights plank. After a great deal of effort by Nixon forces, the Platform Committee reconsidered their previous action and eventually worked out a compromise acceptable to forces on both sides. Their work done, a tired and disgruntled group of delegates were able to relax and join the Convention. They probably never read the platform again.[18]

[18] Professors Karl Lamb and John Kessel have described the 1960 platform development in Tillett (ed.), pp. 39–84.

In 1964, the platform again became a center of controversy. The moderates intended to make the Committee on Resolutions a battleground between themselves and Senator Goldwater. Governors Scranton, Rockefeller, and Romney, all urged that strong planks be written on civil rights and condemning extremists groups. The Committee on Resolutions resoundingly rejected the moderates' proposals and the conflict shifted to the Convention floor.

Five amendments to the platform were offered to the Convention on Tuesday, July 14, 1964. The amendments would have expanded the civil rights section of the platform, two would have condemned extremists groups (one by naming the Communist Party, the Ku Klux Klan, and the John Birch Society), and one would have stated that the President is solely responsible for the use of nuclear weapons. The Goldwater forces opposed all the amendments as unnecessary. They viewed the amendments as attacks on the Senator. They were determined not to compromise on any issue—a mistake they thought Senator Taft had made in 1952. After considerable late-hour debate (the entire platform was read, so it was after 3:00 A.M. in the East when the platform was voted on), all five amendments were defeated. There was only one roll-call vote, that coming on one of the civil rights amendments. The Goldwater forces won by a 2–1 margin—an indication that the Senator was in full command of the meeting.

The Convention in Session

The first days of a Convention are normally rather dull. In general, the party is still in the process of having the Convention take over its functions. The National Committee Chairman calls the meeting to order and the first session is devoted to organizational matters. The National Chairman announces the temporary organization of the Convention, including the Temporary Chairman, Secretary, Parliamentarian, sergeants at arms, doorkeepers, pages, and the Reading Clerk. All but the Temporary Chairman will normally become permanent officials. The membership of the various standing committees is also announced.

The keynote address is delivered in the evening session of the first day, usually by the Temporary Chairman of the Convention (see Table 3–2). On the second day, reports of the Committees on Credentials, Rules and Order of Business, and Permanent Organization are presented. With the adoption of these reports, the Convention is a going concern. The delegates are listed on the permanent roll, the rules are in force, and the Convention has a permanent organization. The Permanent Convention Chairman often has been the Republican Party leader in the House of Representatives in recent years (see Table 3–2), although not in 1964. The rules governing the Convention have traditionally been those of the House of Representatives.

The Resolutions Committee may present the platform on either the second or third day of the Convention. In 1964, the platform was scheduled for the second day. Of course, there are countless speeches by former Presidents and party figures interspersed throughout these proceedings. In between the speeches and other proceedings, entertainers sing and dance to keep the home viewer entertained.

All of the Convention preliminaries are necessary for several reasons. First, the party wants to provide time so that the various presidential candidates can work for delegate support. Second, the program is planned to build toward a climax. The more mundane matters are handled in the first days; then the platform is considered, the nominations are made, and the roll is called for voting on nominations. Third, as already noted, there are certain formalities that must occur so that the Convention will be able to perform its function as chief agent of the party.

Convention campaigning is a fascinating process. The major candidates have already garnered most of their delegate support by Convention time. It is a risky strategy indeed to wait until the Convention before collecting delegate votes. Thus, the efforts of the major contenders are directed toward keeping their delegates in line, working on uncommitted delegates, and where delegates are committed to other candidates, trying for subsequent ballot support (second, third, and so forth). Most of this activity proceeds with only limited fanfare through meetings, phone calls, visits to delegations. There is another level of activity, however, that is as noisy as the first is quiet. The contender's supporters are charged with the responsibility of insuring that the delegates, alternates, convention-goers, and television viewers, know what their man looks like, what he thinks, and how boisterous his followers are. They must perform constantly and they are eager to do so. Pep rallies, posters, parties, parades, pretty girls, preposterous buttons, all characterize this ballyhoo. To many people, such activity *is* the Convention.

Even when the choice for the nomination is obvious, there is considerable Convention campaigning. First, there are literally hundreds of Republicans at presidential nominating conventions who are running for office. Senatorial, gubernatorial, congressional candidates—

all want to take advantage of the opportunity to be seen on national television. And the party wants them to be seen. Thus the home viewer is treated to a parade of the party's best—some delivering principal addresses, some making nominating or seconding speeches, some reading sections of the platform. Second, certain individuals may take the opportunity to launch a campaign to win the nomination four years hence. Both Rockefeller and Goldwater had campaign headquarters at the 1960 convention; the latter was particularly active. Scranton's 1964 activity was viewed by some as a 1968 strategy. Third, if the presidential nomination is settled but not the vice-presidential, various candidates may take the opportunity to advertise themselves. Most of these candidates are well aware that they will not be selected as the running mate. In 1960, the supporters of Representative Gerald Ford, Jr. (Michigan) were particularly active in advertising their man. Fred Seaton (running for Governor of Nebraska), and Walter Judd (running for reelection to the House from Minnesota) also had vigorous backers. And, fourth, the obvious choice for the nomination will likely kick off his effort to win in November with Convention campaigning.

The Battle of the Ballots

Most Republican National Conventions select the presidential candidate without a serious contest. Of the 28 candidates nominated by the Republican Party for the Presidency to 1964, 18 were nominated on the first ballot (see Tables 3–3 and 3–4). James A. Garfield was nominated on the thirty-sixth ballot, the greatest number in the party's history. In this century, only the nominations of Charles Evans Hughes (3), Warren G. Harding (10), Wendell Willkie (6), and Thomas E. Dewey in 1948 (3), required more than one ballot.

The number of ballots alone does not determine whether or not there is conflict at the Convention. There might be intensive conflict that is resolved in one ballot or there might be little conflict and yet, perhaps due to a lack of outstanding candidates, the Convention might cast more than one ballot. In examining the conventions in this century, it is possible to classify them by the degree of conflict and the number of ballots.[19]

---

[19] By a high degree of conflict, I mean a situation in which there are major contenders who have some realistic possibility of mounting a serious challenge to the leading contender.

Table 3–2. Republican National Convention Officials, 1900–1964

Year	Place	National Chairman	Temporary Chairman	Permanent Chairman
1900	Philadelphia	Mark Hanna, Ohio	Edward Wolcott, Colorado	Henry Cabot Lodge, Massachusetts
1904	Chicago	Henry Payne, Wisconsin	Elihu Root, New York	Joseph Cannon, Illinois
1908	Chicago	Harry New, Indiana	Julius Burrows, Michigan	Henry Cabot Lodge, Massachusetts
1912	Chicago	Victor Rosewater, Nebraska	Elihu Root, New York	Elihu Root, New York
1916	Chicago	Charles Hilles, New York	Warren G. Harding, Ohio	Warren G. Harding, Ohio
1920	Chicago	Will Hays, Indiana	Henry Cabot Lodge, Massachusetts	Henry Cabot Lodge, Massachusetts
1924	Cleveland	John Adams, Iowa	Theodore Burton, Ohio	Frank Mondell, Wyoming
1928	Kansas City	William Butler, Massachusetts	Simeon D. Fess, Ohio	George Moses, New Hampshire
1932	Chicago	Simeon D. Fess, Ohio	L. J. Dickinson, Iowa	Bertrand Snell, New York
1936	Cleveland	Henry Fletcher, Rhode Island	Frederick Steiner, Oregon	Bertrand Snell, New York

Table 3–2. (continued)

Year	Place	National Chairman	Temporary Chairman	Permanent Chairman
1940	Philadelphia	John Hamilton, Iowa	Harold Stassen, Minnesota	Joseph Martin, Jr., Massachusetts
1944	Chicago	Harrison Spangler, Iowa	Earl Warren, California	"
1948	Philadelphia	Carroll Reece, Tennessee	Dwight Green, Illinois	"
1952	Chicago	Guy Gabrielson, New Jersey	Walter S. Hallanan, West Virginia	"
			Douglas MacArthur, Keynoter	
1956	San Francisco	Leonard Hall, New York	William Knowland, California	"
			Arthur Langlie, Washington, Keynoter	
1960	Chicago	Thruston B. Morton, Kentucky	Cecil Underwood, West Virginia	Charles Halleck, Indiana
			Walter Judd, Minnesota, Keynoter	
1964	San Francisco	William E. Miller, New York	Mark Hatfield, Oregon	Thruston B. Morton, Kentucky

Source: *Official Convention Program*, Republican National Convention, 1952.

As Table 3–3 shows, 12 of the 17 Republican Party National Conventions in this century made the decision for the candidate with relatively low conflict within the party. Ten of these have settled the matter in one ballot; in 5 of the 10, the party was merely reconfirming its present leadership (1900, 1904, 1924, 1932, and 1956). In 1916, Charles Evans Hughes was nominated in three ballots. He led seven other candidates on the first ballot, none of whom was able to mount any serious threat to his effort to capture the nomination. The 1916 Republican Convention, however, was almost a sideshow. The main attraction was the Progressive Party Convention, since they again nominated Theodore Roosevelt. Would the Republican Party again go down to defeat because of its internal split? Roosevelt stunned his supporters by declining to be their candidate. As Malcolm Moos notes: "More than a few would leave the Republican party for good, and more importantly they would carry thousands away with them. . . . Many of their sons . . . were active leaders in the Democratic party only a generation distant. Many Progressives, including Harold Ickes, supported Hughes that fall, but did so with the feeling that this might be the last trip."[20] Thus the 1916 Republican Convention was characterized by minimal conflict, but the party itself was still suffering from the schism of 1912.

Table 3–3. Classification of Republican Party National Conventions, 1900–1964

Degree of Conflict	Number of Ballots		Totals
	One	More than One	
Low	1900, 1904, 1908, 1924, 1928, 1932, 1936, 1944, 1956, 1960	1916, 1948	12
High	1912, 1952, 1964	1920, 1940	5
Totals	13	4	17

I have also classified the 1948 Republican Convention as one of low conflict. There are no doubt those who will disagree with this classification, but no candidate was able to challenge Governor Thomas E. Dewey seriously. On the first ballot he had almost twice as many votes as his closest rival, Senator Robert A. Taft. All efforts to stop Dewey failed and he smashed home on the third ballot.

[20] Moos, p. 292.

Republicans were reluctant, of course, to select Dewey. They had never before in their history renominated a defeated candidate. There were major contenders for the nomination—more serious contenders than in 1916—but, in my view, Dewey was able to win the nomination with relatively little opposition.

The three conventions in which serious conflict was settled with only one ballot, might well be classified as the most divisive conventions for the party in this century. In 1912, William Howard Taft was renominated on the first ballot, but the party was rent by the conflict between his supporters and those of Theodore Roosevelt. Roosevelt and his group convened immediately following adjournment of the Republican Convention in a hall just a mile from where Taft had been nominated. A third party was formed, the Progressive, or Bull Moose, Party, to nominate Roosevelt. Both parties were routed in the Electoral College, though together they polled more popular votes than did Woodrow Wilson.

By 1952, the Republican Party had developed a different habit. They had built a tradition in the 1930's and 1940's of selecting the more progressive candidates. Another Taft—the son of the former President—had become "Mr. Republican" and "Mr. Conservative." His record in the United States Senate was much admired by his followers. He had twice been a serious candidate for the Republican nomination, 1940 and 1948, and seemed to be the logical choice by 1952. He could argue in his behalf that though the party had been shying away from more conservative candidates, the party continued to go down to defeat, even when victory seemed assured, for example, in 1948. Taft worked hard to win the nomination before the convention and came to Chicago with nearly enough delegate support to carry him to victory. But those who had been successful in nominating Republican candidates in recent years were not satisfied with Taft. They convinced General Eisenhower to try for the nomination, and so "Mr. Republican" was again denied the nomination.

To say that Taft's supporters were disgruntled in 1952 is to understate grossly their real feelings. In 1964, however, the conservatives triumphed. The moderates were split before the convention among several candidates. Senator Goldwater's supporters were intent on preventing another "1952" by developing a strong organization which would prevent any last-minute coalitions strong enough to deny their man the nomination. Nothing was left to chance. Even when it was apparent that Goldwater was assured of the nomination, his strategists continued to seek delegate support and insure that no Goldwater delegate defected to other candidates. The Goldwater organization established in San Francisco the most extensive communications network ever assembled at a national convention.[21] Goldwater's victory over the moderates—as with Eisenhower's victory over the conservatives in 1952—was complete and left the Republican Party as divided as ever between the moderates and the conservatives.

The other two conventions in which there was maximal conflict for the nomination were equally exciting as those noted above, but perhaps less serious for the party. In 1920, a deadlock developed between General Leonard Wood and Governor Frank Lowden of Illinois. After it become clear that neither man could capture enough votes to get the nomination, the Convention turned to Warren G. Harding, nominating him on the tenth ballot.

The 1940 Republican Convention was as exciting as any that either party has had, or may ever have. It was an intense battle in many ways, but it also had an element of "good clean fun." As has been emphasized herein, it is often the case that a logical candidate emerges between conventions. None did between 1936 and 1940. Governor Alfred M. Landon certainly could not be chosen again. He captured only 8 electoral votes in 1936. Governor Dewey was developing as a presidential contender but, as is so well described by Conrad Joyner in his book *The Republican Dilemma,* Dewey had not matured as a contender.[22] The same could be said about Senator Taft. Senator Arthur Vandenburg (Michigan) never really worked for the nomination. Thus the stage was set for an unbelieveable drama and the "rumpled Hoosier," Wendell Willkie, was capable of giving staid Republicans enough drama to last them for a long, long time. Willkie came to the Convention with very few delegate votes but his star was rising; the other candidates were either declining in strength or leveling off. Through five frenzied ballots, Willkie continued to gain support. The tension in the Convention Hall defies description. The galleries were packed with Willkie boosters—all shouting "We Want Willkie." On the sixth ballot, they got their wish.

[21] For a description of another elaborate communications network—that of Kennedy at the Democratic Convention in 1960—see the article by Fred Burke in Paul Tillett (ed.), *Inside Politics: The National Convention, 1960* (Dobbs Ferry, N.Y.: Oceana, 1960), pp. 25–54. Goldwater's strategists are said to have patterned their network after that of Kennedy.

[22] Conrad Joyner, *The Republican Dilemma* (Tucson, Ariz.: University of Arizona Press, 1963), Ch. 2. See also Donald Johnson, *The Republican Party and Wendell Willkie* (Urbana, Ill.: University of Illinois Press, 1960).

Republicans thought that they had nominated a winner but it was the Democrats, in renominating Roosevelt, who again had the winner.

Table 3—4. Republican Party Presidential and Vice-Presidential Candidates, 1856–1964

Year	Presidential Candidate	Number of Ballots	Vice-Presidential Candidate	Number of Ballots
1856	John C. Fremont	2	William Dayton	2
1860*	Abraham Lincoln	3	Hannibal Hamlin	2
1864*	Abraham Lincoln	1	Andrew Johnson	1
1868*	Ulysses S. Grant	1	Schuyler Colfax	5
1872*	Ulysses S. Grant	1	Henry Wilson	1
1876*	Rutherford B. Hayes	7	William Wheeler	Acclamation
1880*	James A. Garfield	36	Chester A. Arthur	1
1884	James G. Blaine	4	John A. Logan	1
1888*	Benjamin Harrison	8	Levi P. Morton	1
1892	Benjamin Harrison	1	Whitelaw Reid	Acclamation
1896*	William McKinley	1	Garrett A. Hobart	1
1900*	William McKinley	1	Theodore Roosevelt	1
1904*	Theodore Roosevelt	1	Charles Fairbanks	Acclamation
1908*	William H. Taft	1	James S. Sherman	1
1912	William H. Taft	1	James S. Sherman	1
1916	Charles E. Hughes	3	Charles Fairbanks	1
1920*	Warren G. Harding	10	Calvin Coolidge	1
1924*	Calvin Coolidge	1	Charles G. Dawes	3
1928*	Herbert Hoover	1	Charles Curtis	1
1932	Herbert Hoover	1	Charles Curtis	1
1936	Alfred M. Landon	1	Frank Knox	1
1940	Wendell L. Willkie	6	Charles L. McNary	1
1944	Thomas E. Dewey	1	John W. Bricker	1
1948	Thomas E. Dewey	3	Earl Warren	Acclamation
1952*	Dwight D. Eisenhower	1	Richard M. Nixon	1
1956*	Dwight D. Eisenhower	1	Richard M. Nixon	1
1960	Richard M. Nixon	1	Henry C. Lodge	1
1964	Barry M. Goldwater	1	William E. Miller	1

Source: *Official Convention Program,* Republican National Convention.

* Indicates that the Republican candidates won the Presidency and Vice-Presidency.

Nominating a Vice-Presidential Candidate

Until recently, the Vice-President was the forgotten man in American politics. Many politicians have declined to run for the office; those who have held the office have had little good to say about it (Vice-President John Nance Garner likened it to a "pitcher of warm spit"), and the office has through the ages been the butt of jokes and satire. I will wager that many readers will find a number of unfamiliar names among Republican vice-presidential candidates in Table 3–4. Some of those unfamiliar names—for example, Schuyler Colfax, Henry Wilson, William Wheeler, Levi P. Morton, and Garrett A. Hobart—actually held the office of Vice-President. In selecting a candidate, the rule has traditionally been that the presidential candidate should have the right to select whomever he wants. Generally, the presidential candidate has wanted a man whom he thinks will mend rifts in the party and/or will help the ticket to win in the general election.

Republicans have followed the rules for nominating a vice-presidential candidate. Twenty-five of the 28 Republican candidates have been nominated on the first ballot or by acclamation (see Table 3–4). The exceptions have occurred when the presidential candidate did not name a man (Grant did not in 1868; Schuyler Colfax finally won on the fifth ballot) and when the first choice would not accept the nomination (Henry Davis refused in 1860, so Hannibal Hamlin was chosen on the second ballot; neither Senator William E. Borah nor Governor Frank Lowden would accept in 1924, so Charles Dawes was nominated on the third ballot).

It should be noted that Republicans should be rather careful in selecting their vice-presidential nominee, since four have succeeded to the Presidency: Andrew Johnson, Chester Arthur, Theodore Roosevelt, and Calvin Coolidge. One, Richard Nixon, very nearly became President when Eisenhower had a severe heart attack.

Summary

Most nominations for public office in the Republican Party occur as a result of primary elections. This peculiarly American method of nomination is basically "antiparty" in the sense of formally denying the party of an important source of strength. In fact, of course, political parties have been able to work around this device and retain a high degree of control over candidacies.

The most spectacular of the nominations in America is that for the Presidency. The primary has even invaded this event in some states, but the formal nomination still occurs in a convention. The convention is mostly a marvelous spectacle. The "man who" has already been determined. On those occasions in modern times, when the choice was not obvious, party strife has resulted.

CHAPTER 4

Electing Republicans

THE PAYOFF FOR A POLITICAL PARTY is at the polls. The nominating Convention is a truly great rally, but the rallying spirit for a party has to be fed with occasional victories. Fortunately for the Republican Party, the Convention meets three and one-half years after the general election. If it were to follow immediately the first Tuesday after the first Monday in November, the Republican Party might well have disappeared as a national party.

In this chapter, I shall focus on Republican efforts to win elections and the problems they face in doing so. As before, I shall relate the strategy of Republican campaigning to the fact that their party is the minority party in the nation.

American Voting Behavior—Challenge to Republican Candidates

The most outstanding characteristic of the American voting public from the point of view of Republican presidential candidates is that there are more Americans of voting age who prefer the Democratic Party than those who prefer the Republican Party. The Survey Research Center (SRC) at the University of Michigan has established that an overwhelming majority of voters has a "lasting attachment" to one of the parties.[1] In October 1960, 54 per cent of the respondents in an SRC survey indicated a preference for the Democratic Party, 34 per cent for the Republican Party. The remaining 12 per cent were either Independents, apolitical, or didn't know which party they preferred. The figures do not vary greatly between 1952 and 1960. Most students agree that the Republican disadvantage among voters is roughly 3 to 2. Thus a Democratic candidate can campaign within his party—that is, for votes of those people who identify with the Democratic Party. A Republican candidate *must* campaign for Independent and Democratic voters.

One cannot take for granted that just because there is a 3 to 2 edge for Democrats in stated party loyalty of American voters, that Republicans will lose all elections, or even presidential elections, by a

[1] Angus Campbell, *et al., The American Voter* (New York: Wiley, 1960), p. 121.

60–40 vote split. Obviously, in certain sections of the United States, Republicans hold an edge in party preference among voters. In the South, on the other hand, Democrats are in the vast majority. Further, as Donald E. Stokes has noted, there are certain characteristics of those people who identify with the Republican Party which modify the Democratic advantage. Stokes discusses the "greater psychological involvment of the average Republican in politics."[2] This difference in involvement between those identifying with the two parties has two important effects: First, Republicans are more likely than Democrats to vote. Second, Republicans are less likely to defect to the other party than are Democrats. Thus a more accurate estimate of the Republican Party's expected share of the vote in presidential elections, according to the Survey Research Center, is 46 per cent or 47 per cent rather than 40 per cent.[3]

How was it that a Republican was elected President in 1952 and 1956 when a majority of voters indicated a preference for the Democratic Party? And why was it that after winning in 1952 and 1956, the Republicans lost the 1960 presidential election? The Survey Research Center suggests four basic categories of presidential elections.[4] The first of these is the maintaining election. As noted before, there are long periods when one party is dominant. When there is congruence between the basic partisan attachment of the voters and their vote for President, the party preferred by a majority of voters will win. Such elections are classified by SRC as *maintaining* elections. Since 1932, the partisan preference split has favored the Democrats. Thus, when Democrats are returned to the White House, the election falls into this first category (see Table 4–1).

The second category includes those elections where the partisan attachment among voters remains roughly the same, but short-term factors result in voters crossing party lines to vote for the other party's candidate. If enough voters cross over, that is, vote contrary to their partisan preference, the minority party candidate wins. These elections are labeled *deviating* elections. Note that *the division of partisan loyalties does not change markedly in such elections*. Thus Democrats vote for the Republican candidate without actually changing their party loyalty.

[2] Donald E. Stokes, "1960 and the Problem of Deviating Elections," Paper delivered at the 1961 Annual Meeting of the American Political Science Association, St. Louis, Missouri, September 6–9, 1961, p. 4.

[3] Stokes, p. 5.

[4] Campbell, *et al.*, Ch. 19.

When the majority party, that is, the party which is preferred by a majority of the voters, recaptures control of the White House, there is a *reinstatement* of congruity between partisan loyalty and presidential voting. In this circumstance the election is labeled a *reinstating* election—the third category.

Finally, as has been emphasized several times, there are periods when some voters actually change their partisan loyalties, and new voters (young persons reaching voting age and older persons who vote for the first time) no longer split in favor of the majority party, but favor the second party. Such changes have been associated with major national crises—for example, the Civil War and the Depression. Presidential elections that demonstrate this basic change are labeled *realigning* elections—the fourth category suggested by the Survey Research Center.

Table 4–1 classifies presidential elections during this century. Note that minority party victories are always *deviating* elections. Thus Eisenhower's victories in 1952 and 1956 were the result of incongruity between various short-term factors and the partisan loyalty of many Democrats to their party. These short-term factors include the candidates, the issues, the record of the two parties, and the groups involved in politics. Any individual voter has attitudes on these "political objects" in a campaign. The great majority of voters also are equipped with basic partisan loyalty. There may well be conflict between partisan loyalty and the voter's attitudes toward the candidates, issues, and so on. There was such conflict for many Democrats in 1952 and 1956. Though there was a pro-Democratic attitude on some of the short-term factors, the overall result was a pro-Republican attitude among voters. Particularly important in both years was the favorable attitude among voters toward Eisenhower as a candidate and (to a somewhat lesser extent) toward the Republican posture on foreign affairs. In 1952, there was also a strong anti-Democratic attitude toward the parties as managers of government.

Thus a Republican candidate won in 1952 and 1956 because many Democratic partisans perceived incongruity between their party loyalty and certain objects of the immediate campaign. But this conflict did not result in their changing their party—only their presidential vote! Thus, it is not possible to classify the 1952–1956 period as a *realigning* era, similar to 1932–1936. No doubt some Democrats did change their party loyalty, but the voting public in 1960 still was characterized by a pro-Democratic partisan alignment.

Table 4–1. Classification of Presidential Elections, 1900–1964

| Category[a] | Party Winning | | Total Number in Category |
	Republican	Democrat	
Maintaining	1900, 1904, 1908, 1924, 1928	1940, 1944, 1948	8
Deviating	1952, 1956	1912, 1916	4
Reinstating	1920	1960	2
Realigning	—	1932, 1936[b]	2
Totals	8	8	16

a The categories used here are those developed by the Survey Research Center in Angus Campbell, *et al., The American Voter* (New York: Wiley, 1960), Chapter 19. See also Philip Converse, *et al.,* "Stability and Change in 1960: A Reinstating Election," *American Political Science Review,* Vol. LV (June, 1961), pp. 269–280.

b One might also categorize 1936 as a "maintaining" election. SRC, however, makes the point that the Democrats reached their peak in 1936—thus, that election was the capstone of the realignment.

Even if Nixon had won in 1960, therefore, the election would have been classified as a *deviating* election. Further substantiation for this analysis results from an examination of how well other Republicans fared in elections during the 1952–1960 period. Congressional Republicans continued to lose so that by 1958 they were a 2–1 minority in both houses of Congress. As is emphasized by the Survey Research Center, the minority party cannot hope to continue winning the White House over an extended period of time unless there is realignment of basic partisan loyalties among the voting public.

Who are those Americans who do state a preference for the Republican Party? If there were a simple answer to that question, and only Republicans knew the answer, campaigning would be much easier for the party. Unfortunately the answer that is available is rather imprecise from the point of view of the Republican campaigner. The Survey Research Center, the Bureau of Applied Social Research at Columbia, and other research and polling organizations have delineated certain broad sociological and economic differences between those who align themselves with the two parties. Though these differences are of interest to the campaigner, he would like to know precisely where his support is, where his opponent's support is, and where the waverers are.

If such demographic variables as age, sex, income, place of residence, education, occupation, religion, and race are correlated with party vote for President, the following groups have tended to vote Republican.[5]

Age: Older more than younger.

Sex: Women more than men.

Income: Higher income more than lower income.

Place of
residence: Suburban, town and rural areas more than central city.

Education: College educated more than high school or grade school educated.

Occupation: Professional, business, and white collar more than skilled and unskilled workers.

Religion: Protestant more than Catholic or Jewish.

Race: White more than Negro.

Note that the above groups *tend* to vote Republican—that is, Republican candidates have been able to garner a greater proportion of the vote in those groups. This is not to say that many whites, Protestants, and professional men, for example, do not vote Democratic, nor that many men, skilled workers, and Catholics do not vote Republican. Further, Republican candidates can depend on some of their supporting groups more than on others. Thus they get consistently high percentages from those with annual incomes over $5,000 (68 per cent in 1948, 67 per cent in 1952, and 62 per cent in 1956 according to the SRC), whereas the Republican share of the women's vote, or of rural votes, is much less consistently high.

Professor Clinton Rossiter best summarizes all of the rather dull statistics on demographic differences in voting for the two parties. After warning of the problems in generalizing on this subject, he notes that "the Democrats are a party of the South, the city, the poor, the unions, the hard-luck farmers, the immigrants and their children,

[5] The principal voting studies are Paul Lazarsfeld, *et al., The People's Choice* (New York: Duell, Sloan & Pearce, 1944); Bernard Berelson, *et al., Voting* (Chicago: University of Chicago Press, 1954); Angus Campbell and R. L. Kahn, *The People Elect a President* (Ann Arbor, Mich.: Institute for Social Research, 1952); Campbell, *et al., The Voter Decides* (Evanston, Ill.: Row, Peterson, 1954); Campbell, *et al., The American Voter* (New York: Wiley, 1960). The summary of voting tendencies among groups is based on findings in these various studies.

Negroes, white supremacists, the young, the least educated, and the most educated; the Republicans a party of the North, the country, suburbia, the rich, the middle class, the business community, the good-luck farmers, the old stock, the middle-aged, and the college graduates."[6] It so happens that, when totaled, there are more of the former than there are of the latter.

One final observation about the significance of American voting behavior for the Republican Party should be made. Following a realigning era, the party which is tagged with the responsibility for whatever crisis caused realignment will probably have great difficulty in altering its image. The Republican Party has had to live with the "Great Depression" for a long, long time. In 1952, the SRC discovered at least three "marks" of the Depression on the party. First, the Republican Party was still viewed as the party of Depression by many voters. Second, the Democratic Party was perceived as the abler of the two parties for solving domestic problems, and third, the Republican Party was identified as the party of high status groups.[7] Between 1952 and 1956, the Eisenhower Administration was successful in modifying the first two perceptions, but not the third. In 1960, Democratic candidate Kennedy revived the Depression stigma and spoke often of the domestic policy record of the Republican Party.

Presidential Campaigns

The political campaign in America is a curious phenomenon. In theory, it should be the time in which the representative and his constituents come together to review the record and discuss upcoming issues. In fact, it seems to be a time in which candidates race about their constituency—whether it is the nation or a congressional district—in frenzied effort to project a favorable image so that voters will (1) go to the polls, (2) find the candidate's name on the ballot, and (3) vote for that name.

Republican presidential candidates must face a number of unpleasant facts of life. First, as just discussed, there are more Americans who prefer the Democratic Party. Second, America is enjoying a period of prosperity; there is no depression likely which might

[6] Clinton Rossiter, *Parties and Politics in America* (Ithaca, N.Y.: Cornell University Press, 1960), p. 105.

[7] See Angus Campbell, *et al.*, *The American Voter* (New York: Wiley, 1960), p. 45 and Ch. 7, for full discussion of the effect of the Depression.

realign party preferences. Third, money will not win a presidential election, but lack of it may lose one. Fourth, the Republican Party is most highly organized in those sections of the country that are losing population. Thus the candidate will not win by appealing only to Republican voters. He is denied any strong issues upon which to base a campaign. He can't buy the election and he can't rely on the party as currently organized.

How can the Republican Party overcome these handicaps? Perhaps it is not possible to plan to do so but, fortunately for the survival of the two-party system, one will never convince either party officials or presidential candidates of that. Let's examine the various phases of a Republican presidential campaign and illustrate these phases with what happened in the 1960 election.

There are basically four phases to the campaign. The first might be called the *nominating* phase. Formerly this would not be identified as a phase of the campaign; it was simply party business. The development of the mass media, however, leads me to include the nominating period as a campaign phase. The nominating convention is a television spectacle. The party and its candidate have a golden opportunity to get a great deal of exposure. Further, studies show that many people actually decide how they will vote at the time of the convention.[8] Thus the party must put on a good show in beginning its campaign.

Another reason for including the nominating period as a campaign phase is that the Republican Party decision on who their candidate will be is of importance in determining whether there will be a Republican in the White House. One may expect that Republican presidential candidates will be successful if they are able to woo independent voters and Democrats. And their success in winning these votes may well depend on whether the candidate himself is strongly identified with the Republican Party or not. In a period of Democratic Party dominance, Republicans win only when Democrats *deviate* and vote the other party. Democrats are likely to be attracted to the Republican candidate if they are able to identify with him. They are unlikely to identify with him if he is a strongly partisan Republican, or if they are perfectly able to identify with

8 See the summary figures presented in Austin Ranney and Willmoore Kendall, *Democracy and The American Party System* (New York: Harcourt, Brace & World, 1956), p. 353, which show that 28 per cent of all voters made their decision at the time of the convention in 1948 and 34 per cent did so in 1952.

their own candidate. Eisenhower was not identified strongly either as a politician or a Republican. Nixon was identified as both. Even though Nixon appealed to Americans to rise above party politics during a time of crisis and vote the man, not the party, he had long since been identified as a partisan Republican.

If the Democrats are successful in selecting a presidential candidate with whom Democrats can identify, then the Republican candidate will have difficulty winning. For a variety of reasons, Governor Stevenson was a man with whom Democrats had trouble identifying.[9] John F. Kennedy, on the other hand, was popular among most Democrats, particularly northern Democrats. And Kennedy made every effort during the campaign to project an image of himself in the tradition of the Democratic "greats"—notably Franklin D. Roosevelt and Woodrow Wilson.

If the party's choice of presidential candidate is obvious, and it usually is, then pre-convention activity is also important to the campaign. In 1960, Nixon was the only possible candidate. Thus he was able to concentrate very early on organizing, planning, and financing his campaign. Even if the party's choice is not obvious, the pre-convention activity may be significant. For example, in 1952, Eisenhower was able to test and increase his popularity during the spring months.

The second phase in the campaign cycle is the *planning,* or *strategy,* phase. It takes place immediately after the Convention, when the nation is taking a breather from politics and is reabsorbed in baseball and summer vacations. Normally, the month of August constitutes the planning phase. As indicated above, if the Convention is merely ratifying its only alternative, the planning phase starts much earlier. By August, however, the Republican candidate knows who his opponent will be and this fact is of utmost importance in mapping strategy.

In 1960, Nixon was rather certain that Kennedy would be his opponent and therefore was able to develop strategy accordingly. He no doubt was as surprised as the rest of the nation when Senator Lyndon B. Johnson was selected as the running mate, but no major changes in strategy were necessary. Nixon could pledge to a cheering convention that the "campaign begins tonight, here and now . . ." and that he would "carry this campaign into every one of the fifty

[9] For some of these reasons, see Campbell, *et al., The American Voter,* p. 58.

states . . ." Thus Nixon indicated in his acceptance speech at the Republican Convention that his strategy was already mapped and that he would telescope the August planning phase considerably. True to his word, the Republican candidate visited six states within ten days of receiving the nomination.

It is appropriate at this juncture to discuss campaign organization. The weak position of the National Committee in relation to state and local organizations means that the candidate himself must fashion a campaign organization. Since the National Committee lacks the power to integrate all of the multitudinous party organizational units, the candidate has to develop an integrating force of his own. Nixon collected the most able political minds in the party in his "Plans Board".[10] Members of the Board were Leonard Hall, Campaign Chairman; Robert Finch, Campaign Director; James Bassett, Planning Director; Thruston Morton, National Committee Chairman; Richard Guylay, Publicity Director of the National Committee; Carroll Newton, Director of Television Operations; and Robert Merriam, liaison with the White House. In addition, Nixon had other personal aides—notably Herbert Klein, his press secretary. Despite the potential effectiveness of this organization, Nixon reportedly did not rely on it to any great extent. For the most part, he made the decisions regarding his campaign, and many of the experts had no chance to implement their ideas.[11]

What sort of decisions have to be made in the planning phase? The problems are limitless. The candidate must decide where to concentrate his efforts. Nixon pledged to campaign in all fifty states but, of course, he spent more time in states with a large electoral vote—principally California, Illinois, Wisconsin, Minnesota, Ohio, New York, Pennsylvania, and Florida. The candidate must decide which issues to emphasize. Nixon stressed foreign relations. He is faced with decisions about raising money, utilizing the various mass media, and establishing a campaign schedule. He must consider the best possible use of his running mate and other Republican candidates. He must concern himself with pacing the campaign—a problem in which Nixon was especially interested. And he must decide how

---

[10] See Theodore White, *The Making of the President, 1960* (New York: Atheneum, 1961), p. 264, on the Plans Board. This book provides us with one of the most readable accounts of a presidential election ever published. See the Bibliography, pp. 148–153 for other campaign studies.

[11] White, p. 313.

he can best capitalize on his own strength and his opponent's weaknesses.[12]

In the third phase, the *test* phase, of the campaign, candidates have a chance to work out some of the "bugs" in their organization and planning. Generally speaking, this testing occurs in the month of September. The candidate learns something about the effectiveness of his organization and makes changes when necessary. He is able to determine whether certain issues have "punch" and "grab." He engages his opponent for the first time, and, much like the early rounds of a boxing match, tries to sense hitherto unknown weaknesses of his adversary that he will exploit later in the campaign. He is able to test different phrases in an effort to discover a "basic" speech on which he can rely for the remainder of the campaign.

As noted above, Nixon had begun his test phase earlier than Kennedy. First, he was able to do pre-convention planning because he did not have to fight for the nomination, and second, a session of Congress trapped Senator Kennedy in Washington during August. Fate did not continue to be kind to the Vice-President, however. In late August, he injured his kneecap on the door of a car while campaigning in North Carolina. The knee became infected and Nixon was forced to lose nearly two weeks of campaigning. Kennedy, meanwhile, was freed from his prison with the adjournment of Congress and he moved fast and furiously to make up for lost time. The full effect of Nixon's injury on the campaign is difficult to assess, but it was an unscheduled event which undoubtedly forced him to alter his campaign plan. And if Theodore White's analysis is accurate, the injury and Nixon's response to the lost time were of considerable significance.[13]

The fourth and final phase of the campaign might be labeled the *critical* phase. It is a deadly serious part of the campaign. The pattern is set. There is no turning back; major changes in strategy are no longer in order. It is October now, and the candidate increases his activity according to whatever strategy has been evaluated as most effective.

[12] Theodore White discusses such strategic considerations in detail, Ch. 10. See also Nelson W. Polsby and Aaron Wildavsky, *Presidential Elections: Strategies of American Electoral Politics* (New York: Scribner, 1964), Ch. 3.

[13] White states (p. 273) that: ". . . out of impatient impulse, and against the advice of his closest associates, Mr. Nixon proceeded to schedule himself from the hospital bed as if he must make up for lost time by starting the marathon with a sprint."

Though normally Americans are preoccupied with baseball until after the World Series, they were encouraged to attend to politics earlier in the fall of 1960. The critical phase began on September 26 when the two candidates faced off for a debate before a television audience estimated at over 65 million. Kennedy won the set by winning the first debate.[14] He destroyed the effectiveness of one of Nixon's principal strategies—that is, to contrast Kennedy's inexperience and lack of knowledge with his own experience and fund of knowledge. At a time in which major changes in strategy were no longer possible, Kennedy had effectively neutralized, perhaps even capitalized on, a Republican issue. No amount of activity on Nixon's part could recoup following the disaster of September 26. And Nixon tried valiantly. Following the debates, Democrats knew they had a candidate and 1960 was to become a "reinstating election." Many Eisenhower Democrats would once again vote their party preference.

Congressional Campaigns

Most of the research that has been done on voting behavior and campaigning has focused on the presidential campaign. When these topics are discussed in the classroom, a possible mistake is to generalize that voting behavior and campaigning are the same for all campaigns. A legitimate hypothesis would seem to be, however, that voters behave differently as they move down the ballot and that candidates campaign differently for different public offices. There are certain obvious differences between the campaign situations of Congressmen, Senators, and Presidents. Differences in scope of the campaign, cost, organization, awareness of the candidate by voters, interparty competition—all are important factors in explaining variations in campaigning.

Since this is a period of Democratic Party dominance at the polls, Republicans have special problems in winning seats in the House and Senate. For a variety of reasons, the incumbent legislator has a campaign advantage and, since 1932, it has been the case that in any one

[14] The Gallup Poll showed that 43 per cent of those who had seen or heard the first debate thought that Kennedy had done the better job, 23 per cent thought Nixon had, 29 per cent thought it was a draw, and 5 per cent had no opinion. See Stanley Kelley, Jr., "The 1960 Presidential Election," *American Government Annual, 1961–1962,* edited by Ivan Hinderaker (New York: Holt, Rinehart & Winston, 1961), pp. 66–67. See also Sidney Kraus (ed.), *The Great Debates: Background, Perspective, Effects* (Bloomington, Ind.: Indiana University Press, 1962).

election there are usually many more Democratic than Republican incumbents. Further, Republican incumbents on the average have lower winning margins than Democratic incumbents. Indeed, many Democrats win reelection with no opposition. Table 4–2 shows that in House races, the Democrats have won a total of 436 seats without opposition in the past six elections—an average of 73 seats an election. Republicans have won only 21 seats without opposition in the six elections—an average of 3.5 seats per election. Of course, most of the seats won by the Democrats are in States in the Deep South, but there are several in other states as well. For example, in 1960, Republicans failed to run candidates in 2 California districts, 3 Kentucky districts, 5 Massachusetts districts, 1 Missouri district, 7 Tennessee districts, and 13 Texas districts. There has been a concerted effort on the part of the Republican Party since 1960 to reduce the number of uncontested congressional seats, even in the Deep South.

Table 4–2. Uncontested Races for Election to the House of Representatives, 1952–1962

Election Year	Democrats Winning	Republicans Winning
1952	80	12
1954	83	2
1956	62	3
1958	88	1
1960	70	2
1962	53	1
Totals	436	21

The situation in the Senate is not so serious for the Republican Party, but even there the campaign challenge is considerable. Between 1952 and 1962 (six elections), 19 Democrats were unopposed for reelection. Only 1 Republican was unopposed. Further, of those victorious Democrats who did have opposition during the six-election period, 37.8 per cent (42 of 111) won by 60 per cent or more of the vote and 18.0 per cent won by 70 per cent or more. Of the victorious Republicans with Democratic opponents, only 18.2 per cent (16 of 88) won by 60 per cent or more of the vote, and none won by 70 per cent or more.

In short, the advantage in a campaign is with the Democrats. They win many seats in the House and Senate without opposition and when they do have opposition, their margin of victory is usually greater. This is not to say that there are no safe Republican districts or states. Indeed, there are, but they are many fewer than for the Democrats.

There are, at a minimum, three basic types of campaign situations for Republican candidates. The first is where a Republican incumbent is seeking reelection. Chances are that he will be reelected (though his chances are somewhat less than for his Democratic counterpart). The second is where there is no incumbent, but a Republican held the seat in the past. In this situation, the Republican candidate has a good chance of winning the seat, depending on the strength of Republican Party organization in the constituency. But he has a more difficult campaign problem than a Republican incumbent. He must acquaint the constituency (state or district) with his name and try to project a favorable image. The third campaign situation is where a Republican is challenging a Democratic incumbent or Democratic Party incumbent candidate (that is, a district where the Democratic incumbent has retired). This Republican has a most depressing assignment. Normally he will not be well known among the voters; he will probably be faced with such problems as poor organization, little money, and voter registration disadvantage. Few of these candidates will win. In House races in 1958, only 1 Republican challenger won; in 1960, 19 won; and in 1962, 8 won (though several Republican incumbents defeated Democratic incumbents where they were thrown together by redistricting in 1962). In Senate races in 1958, no Republican challengers won; in 1960, 1 won; and in 1962, 2 won.

Candidates for both parties employ about the same campaign tactics. In House races, the incumbent makes every effort to project an image of ability and knowledge. He tends to avoid commitments on specific issues, concentrating on developing an organization that will impress voters with his name, his record, and his ability. The precise nature of his campaign organization and his use of specific techniques depend on constituency characteristics.

In Senate races, the incumbent has a somewhat different problem. His name is more likely to be known by the voters so he does not have to spend as much time identifying himself in the political world. On the other hand, his record is probably also better known, so he has to deal with issues in more detail than does his colleague in the House. His campaign organization has to be elaborate and he will rely on every conceivable campaign technique, since his is a heterogenous constituency. He must try to reach all voters. The challengers to Senate and House incumbents frantically search for means to advertise themselves and convince enough voters of reasons for ousting the incumbent.

Election Results Since 1932

How successful have Republican candidates been in the last thirty years? An examination of election results since 1932 provides a summary of the problems and prospects faced by the Republican Party.

Presidential Election Results

The Republican Party has captured the White House on two occasions since 1932—both times with one of the most popular presidential candidates in history. In 1956, President Eisenhower garnered 35,584,346 popular votes, more than did any man in history, and 457 electoral votes, more than did any Republican in history. Eisenhower's two great victories were cause for celebration among Republicans. They had come a long way since 1936 when Republican candidate Alfred M. Landon received 16,679,583 popular votes and only *8 electoral votes* (See Table 4–3).

Table 4–3. Popular and Electoral Vote for President, 1932–1964

Year	Candidates	Popular Vote	Electoral Vote
1932	Roosevelt, D.	22,821,857	472
	Hoover, R.	15,761,841	59
1936	Roosevelt, D.	27,476,673	523
	Landon, R.	16,679,583	8
1940	Roosevelt, D.	27,243,466	449
	Willkie, R.	22,304,755	82
1944	Roosevelt, D.	25,602,505	432
	Dewey, R.	22,006,278	99
1948	Truman, D.	24,104,020	303
	Dewey, R.	21,970,904	189
1952	Stevenson, D.	27,314,992	89
	Eisenhower, R.	33,937,252	442
1956	Stevenson, D.	26,026,158	74
	Eisenhower, R.	35,584,346	457
1960	Kennedy, D.	34,221,349	303
	Nixon, R.	34,108,546	219
1964	Johnson, D.	43,126,218	486
	Goldwater, R.	27,174,898	52

Table 4–4 presents a state-by-state breakdown of Republican success in presidential elections since 1932. The states are ranked according to their support of Republican candidates. Only 10 states have given their electoral votes to the Republican candidate in a majority of the elections, 1932–1964. These 10 states, the most Republican states in presidential elections, have a total of only 59 electoral votes of the 268 needed for election.

Table 4–4. Presidential Vote by States, 1932–1964[a] (States ranked by support of Republican candidate)

State	1932	1936	1940	1944	1948	1952	1956	1960	1964	Number of Elections for Republican
Maine	R	R	R	R	R	R	R	R	D	8
Vermont	R	R	R	R	R	R	R	R	D	8
Indiana	D	D	R	R	R	R	R	R	D	6
Kansas	D	D	R	R	R	R	R	R	D	6
Nebraska	D	D	R	R	R	R	R	R	D	6
North Dakota	D	D	R	R	R	R	R	R	D	6
South Dakota	D	D	R	R	R	R	R	R	D	6
Colorado	D	D	R	R	D	R	R	R	D	5
Iowa	D	D	R	R	D	R	R	R	D	5
New Hampshire	R	D	D	D	R	R	R	R	D	5
Arizona	D	D	D	D	D	R	R	R	R	4
Connecticut	R	D	D	D	R	R	R	D	D	4
Delaware	R	D	D	D	R	R	R	D	D	4
Michigan	D	D	R	D	R	R	R	D	D	4
Ohio	D	D	D	R	D	R	R	R	D	4
Oregon	D	D	D	D	R	R	R	R	D	4
Pennsylvania	R	D	D	D	R	R	R	D	D	4
Wisconsin	D	D	D	R	D	R	R	R	D	4
Wyoming	D	D	D	R	D	R	R	R	D	4
California	D	D	D	D	D	R	R	R	D	3
Florida	D	D	D	D	D	R	R	R	D	3
Idaho	D	D	D	D	D	R	R	R	D	3
Maryland	D	D	D	D	R	R	R	D	D	3
Montana	D	D	D	D	D	R	R	R	D	3
New Jersey	D	D	D	D	R	R	R	D	D	3
New Mexico	D	D	D	D	D	R	R	R	D	3
New York	D	D	D	D	R	R	R	D	D	3
Oklahoma	D	D	D	D	D	R	R	R	D	3

Table 4–4. (continued)

State	1932	1936	1940	1944	1948	1952	1956	1960	1964	Number of Elections for Republican
Tennessee	D	D	D	D	D	R	R	R	D	3
Utah	D	D	D	D	D	R	R	R	D	3
Virginia	D	D	D	D	D	R	R	R	D	3
Washington	D	D	D	D	D	R	R	R	D	3
Illinois	D	D	D	D	D	R	R	D	D	2
Kentucky	D	D	D	D	D	D	R	R	D	2
Louisiana	D	D	D	D	SR	D	R	D	R	2
Massachusetts	D	D	D	D	D	R	R	D	D	2
Minnesota	D	D	D	D	D	R	R	D	D	2
Nevada	D	D	D	D	D	R	R	D	D	2
Rhode Island	D	D	D	D	D	R	R	D	D	2
Texas	D	D	D	D	D	R	R	D	D	2
Alabama	D	D	D	D	SR	D	D	D	R	1
Georgia	D	D	D	D	D	D	D	D	R	1
Mississippi	D	D	D	D	SR	D	D	U	R	1
Missouri	D	D	D	D	D	D	R	D	D	1
South Carolina	D	D	D	D	SR	D	D	D	R	1
West Virginia	D	D	D	D	D	D	R	D	D	1
Arkansas	D	D	D	D	D	D	D	D	D	0
North Carolina	D	D	D	D	D	D	D	D	D	0
Total Number of States won by Republican	6	2	10	12	16	38	42	26	6	

a R–Republican, D–Democrat, SR–States Rights, U–Unpledged. Hawaii and Alaska not inculded.

It is easy indeed to be pessimistic about Republican chances by examining the patterns in Table 4–4. Close examination of the table, however, reveals that between 1948 and the disaster of 1964 there was hope for future Republican candidates. During the Roosevelt years, all but Maine and Vermont were pierced by that popular campaigner. Beginning in 1948, however, Republican candidates began to win a substantial number of electoral votes (189 in 1948) and in the three elections between 1952 and 1960, the Republican candidate won more states than the Democratic candidate (Eisenhower winning 38 and 42, respectively, in 1952 and 1956, and

Nixon winning 26 in 1960). In fact, if those three elections, 1952–1960, are analyzed, it is seen that 25 states supported the Republican candidate in every election. Many of these 25 states have a low electoral vote count, however, and together they fall considerably short of a majority in the Electoral College (221 of the 268 needed in 1964).

A second source of optimism for Republicans is that between 1952 and 1964 they had begun to recapture states that were lost to the Democrats for twenty years. States such as Arizona, California, Idaho, Montana, New Mexico, Utah, and Washington, were all won by the Republican candidate in 1920, 1924, and 1928, and then lost for five consecutive elections. As noted in Table 4–4, all these states supported the Republican candidate during the 1952–1960 period.

Finally, Republicans can, and have, looked to southern and border states for increased support during presidential elections. Florida, Oklahoma, Tennessee, and Virginia have given their electoral votes to the Republican candidate in three recent elections. Kentucky and Texas went Republican in two recent elections. Further, in 1960, partly owing no doubt to the religious issue, Nixon gained highly respectable percentages in several southern states and lost by less than 10,000 votes of nearly 400,000 cast in South Carolina.

Of course, the 1964 presidential election results suggest that optimistic analysis is not in order for the immediate future.

Congressional and Senatorial Election Results

It can be argued that the best indication of the strength of a national party is its representation in Congress, particularly in the House of Representatives. Whereas the Presidency can be won with a popular candidate, congressional seats are won principally with party organization and reinforced by solid partisan support. Since 1932, the Republican Party has organized only two Congresses—the Eightieth and the Eighty-third. The party captured the White House for eight years of the last thirty-two. It has controlled Congress for just four years.

Table 4–5 presents figures showing party divisions in the Senate and the House since 1932. Only in the Eightieth Congress did the Republican Party have a comfortable margin over the Democrats—58 seats in the House and 6 in the Senate. All in all, Republicans have won about 40 per cent of all congressional and senatorial seats at stake since 1932.

The sectional strength of the Republican Party has not varied

Table 4–5. Congressional and Senatorial Seats Won by the Two Major Parties, 1932–1964

| | | House | | | Senate | | |
| | | | Repub. Gain or | | | | Repub. Gain or |
Year	Congress	Demos.	Repubs.	Loss	Demos.	Repubs.	Loss
1932	73rd	313	117	−101	59	36	−12
1934	74th	322	103	− 14	69	25	−11
1936	75th	333	89	− 14	75	17	− 8
1938	76th	262	169	+ 80	69	23	+ 6
1940	77th	267	162	− 7	66	28	+ 5
1942	78th	222	209	+ 47	57	38	+10
1944	79th	243	190	− 19	57	38	0
1946	80th	188	246	+ 56	45	51	+13
1948	81st	263	171	− 75	54	42	− 9
1950	82nd	234	199	+ 28	48	47	+ 5
1952	83rd	213	221	+ 22	47	48	+ 1
1954	84th	232	203	− 18	48	47	− 1
1956	85th	234	201	− 2	49	47	0
1958	86th	283	154	− 47	66	34	−13
1960	87th	263	174	+ 20	64	36	+ 2
1962	88th	259	176	+ 2	68	32	− 4
1964	89th	295	140	− 36	68	32	0

greatly since 1932. The northeastern and midwestern states have always been the areas of greatest strength for Republicans. In 1936, when the party was at its low ebb, only seven state delegations in the House of Representatives were controlled by the Republicans: Kansas, Maine, Massachusetts, Vermont, Michigan, North Dakota, and Wisconsin. Table 4–6 presents data on party control of state delegations in the House of Representatives. Of those 18 state delegations which the Republicans have controlled 10 times or more, 10 are midwestern states, 6 are northeastern, 1 western, and 1 Rocky Mountain.

Several other observations are possible by examining Table 4–6. First, it can be seen that the Democrats have gradually moved into states which traditionally have sent a majority of Republicans to the House. Note, for example, that several of the more solid Republican states elected a majority of Democrats, or an equal number of Democrats, between 1954 and 1960, a period in which there was a Republican President. Even Maine and Vermont were in the Democratic column in 1958. Massachusetts shows a steady trend toward the Democrats following the 1952 election. Second, there are states which show a trend toward Republican dominance. Ohio, normally thought of as a Republican stronghold, has been surprisingly fickle. In those years before 1950, when there was a Democratic trend, Ohio sent a majority of Democrats to the House (1932, 1934, 1936, 1948). Since 1950, however, Ohio has remained in the Republican column, even sending a majority of Republicans to the House in 1958. The state of Washington also demonstrates an increased tendency to send a majority of Republicans to the House, although they continue to send Democrats to the Senate.

The final column in Table 4–6 shows the percentage of House seats that the Republicans won in a state during the thirty-two year period. North Dakota, Vermont, and New Hampshire lead the field for Republicans; those states have a combined total of 5 House seats. Of the states with delegations of 10 or more representatives, the most Republican include the following (ranked from highest to lowest):

Wisconsin	76%
New Jersey	68%
Michigan	63%
Ohio	60%
Massachusetts	58%
Indiana	56%
Pennsylvania	56%
Illinois	51%
California	50%
New York	49%

Among those southern states which the Democrats have traditionally controlled, there is reflected in the percentages some of the recent advances made by Republicans. Kentucky and Tennessee have the largest percentage of Republicans elected between 1932 and 1962, but this reflects the traditional pockets of Republicanism in those states. Tennessee's first and second districts were won by Republicans in every election throughout the period measured. Though the percentages in Florida, North Carolina, Texas, and Virginia appear unimpressive on the surface, they represent the Republicans' greatest hope in the South. No Republicans at all were elected in those states between 1932 and 1952. Since 1952 (that is, in the six elections, 1952–1962) Republicans have fared rather well, winning 12 per cent of the seats in Florida, 10 per cent in North Carolina, 5 per cent in Texas, and 22 per cent in Virginia. With the probable redistricting action to follow the recent congressional districting decision by the Supreme Court (*Wesberry v. Sanders*), Republicans will probably gain even more seats in the South. For example, in 1962 Texas Republican candidates for the House received a combined total of 44 per cent of the vote cast for congressional candidates but got only *9 per cent* of the seats (2 of 24). Any redistricting plan that equalizes population among districts in Texas will likely add Republicans to the Texas congressional delegation.

The 1964 results show inroads into the Deep South but losses were suffered in Texas and Kentucky. It is necessary to wait until the 1966 congressional elections before making a firm judgment as to the significance of these gains for the Republican Party.

At least one reason that election results for Congress do not·favor the Republicans appears to be that once a realignment of majority-minority position has occurred, the new majority party wins House seats because it *has won House seats*. That is, there is little doubt that the incumbent has a great advantage over the challenger. Of those incumbents seeking reelection to the House of Representatives between 1954 and 1960, an average of *93.9 per cent* were victorious. In fact, a sizable majority of congressional districts are represented by the same party for five consecutive elections. A recent study of interparty competition for congressional seats shows that for the period 1932–1940, 69.9 per cent of all congressional districts were always won by the same party; in 1942–1950, 74.0 per cent were always won by the same party; in 1952–1960, 78.2 per cent were always won by the same party.[15] Before 1932, the Republican Party won a majority of these "no party change" districts. That is no longer the case. Table 4–7 offers one measure of the extent of the Republican Party's minority status in the House of Representatives. Note that their most successful decade since the Depression was between 1942 and 1952—not the most recent decade.

[15] Charles O. Jones, "Inter-Party Competition for Congressional Seats," *Western Political Quarterly,* Vol. XVII (September, 1964), pp. 461–476.

Table 4–6. Party Control of State Delegations, House of Representatives, 1932–1962[a] (States ranked by number of years Republicans dominant)

State	\	\	\	\	\	\	\	Years	\	\	\	\	\	\	\	\	Totals			% Total Seats Won by Repubs. 1932–1962
	32	34	36	38	40	42	44	46	48	50	52	54	56	58	60	62	Repub.	Demo.	Even	
Kans.	R	R	R	R	R	R	R	R	R	R	R	R	R	E	R	R	15	0	1	84
N.D.	R	R	R	R	R	R	R	R	R	R	R	R	R	E	R	R	15	0	1	97
Mich.	D	R	R	R	R	R	R	R	R	R	R	R	R	R	R	R	15	1	0	63
Vt.	R	R	R	R	R	R	R	R	R	R	R	R	R	D	R	R	15	1	0	94
Wis.	E	R*	R*	R	R	R	R	R	R	R	R	R	R	E	R	R	14	0	2	76
N.J.	R	R	E	R	R	R	R	R	R	R	R	D	R	R	R	R	14	1	1	68
N.H.	E	E	E	R	R	R	R	R	R	R	R	R	R	R	R	R	13	0	3	91
Me.	D	D	R	R	R	R	R	R	R	R	R	R	D	D	R	R	13	3	0	81
Pa.	R	D	D	R	D	R	R	R	R	R	R	R	R	D	R	R	13	3	0	56
Wyo.	R	D	D	R	D	R	R	R	R	R	R	R	R	R	R	R	13	3	0	81
Ia.	D	D	D	R	R	R	R	R	R	R	R	R	E	E	R	R	12	3	1	79
Minn.	R	R	D	R	R	R	R	R	R	R	R	D	D	R	R	E	12	3	1	63
Neb.	D	D	D	R	R	R	R	R	R	R	R	R	R	E	R	R	12	3	1	70
S.D.	D	D	E	R	R	R	R	R	R	R	R	R	E	E	R	R	11	2	3	78
Mass.	R	R	R	R	E	R	R	R	R	R	R	E	E	D	D	D	11	3	2	58
Ohio	D	D	D	R	R	R	R	R	D	R	R	R	R	R	R	R	11	4	1	60
Ind.	D	D	D	R	D	R	R	R	D	R	R	D	R	D	R	R	11	5	0	56
Ore.	D	D	D	R	R	R	R	R	R	R	R	R	D	D	E	D	10	5	1	68
Ill.	D	D	D	D	R	R	R	R	R	R	R	R	R	D	D	E	9	6	1	51
Wash.	D	D	D	D	D	D	R	R	R	R	R	R	R	R	R	R	9	6	1	52

Table 4–6. (continued)

State	32	34	36	38	40	42	44	46	48	50	52	54	56	58	60	62	Repub.	Demo.	Even	% Total Seats Won by Repubs. 1932–1962
Del.	D	R	D	R	D	R	D	R	R	R	R	D	R	D	D	D	8	8	0	50
N.Y.	D	D	D	D	D	D	R	R	D	R	R	R	R	R	D	R	8	8	0	49
Calif.	D	D	D	D	D	D	D	R	R	R	R	R	R	D	R	D	7	9	0	50
Conn.	E	D	D	D	D	R	D	R	E	R	R	R	R	D	D	D	6	8	2	49
Colo.	D	D	D	D	R	R	R	R	D	E	E	E	E	D	E	E	4	6	6	42
Utah	D	D	D	D	D	D	D	E	D	D	R	R	R	E	D	R	4	10	2	31
Nev.	D	D	D	D	D	D	D	D	D	D	R	R	R	D	D	D	3	13	0	19
Ida.	D	D	E	E	E	E	E	R	E	E	R	D	E	E	D	D	2	5	9	40
Mo.	D	D	D	D	D	D	D	D	D	D	R	R	D	D	D	D	2	14	0	23
Md.	D	D	D	D	D	D	D	D	D	E	R	D	D	D	D	D	1	14	1	22
R.I.	D	D	D	R	D	D	D	D	D	D	D	D	D	D	D	D	1	15	0	3
Mont.	D	D	E	E	E	D	D	D	E	E	E	E	D	D	E	E	0	7	9	28
Ariz.	D	D	D	D	D	D	E	D	E	E	E	E	D	D	D	D	0	11	5	21
N. Mex.	D	D	D	D	D	E	E	E	E	E	D	D	D	D	D	D	0	11	5	19
W. Va.	D	D	D	D	D	D	D	D	D	D	D	D	D	E	E	D	0	14	2	15
Ala.	D	D	D	D	D	D	D	D	D	D	D	D	D	D	D	D	0	16	0	0
Ark.	D	D	D	D	D	D	D	D	D	D	D	D	D	D	D	D	0	16	0	0
Fla.	D	D	D	D	D	D	D	D	D	D	D	D	D	D	D	D	0	16	0	6
Ga.	D	D	D	D	D	D	D	D	D	D	D	D	D	D	D	D	0	16	0	0
Ky.	D	D	D	D	D	D	D	D	D	D	D	D	D	D	D	D	0	16	0	12

Table 4-6. (continued)

State	\	\	\	\	\	\	\	Years	\	\	\	\	\	\	\	\	Totals	\	\	% Total Seats Won by Repubs. 1932–1962
	32	34	36	38	40	42	44	46	48	50	52	54	56	58	60	62	Repub.	Demo.	Even	
La.	D	D	D	D	D	D	D	D	D	D	D	D	D	D	D	D	0	16	0	0
Miss.	D	D	D	D	D	D	D	D	D	D	D	D	D	D	D	D	0	16	0	0
N.C.	D	D	D	D	D	D	D	D	D	D	D	D	D	D	D	D	0	16	0	4
Okla.	D	D	D	D	D	D	D	D	D	D	D	D	D	D	D	D	0	16	0	10
S.C.	D	D	D	D	D	D	D	D	D	D	D	D	D	D	D	D	0	16	0	0
Tenn.	D	D	D	D	D	D	D	D	D	D	D	D	D	D	D	D	0	16	0	22
Tex.	D	D	D	D	D	D	D	D	D	D	D	D	D	D	D	D	0	16	0	2
Va.	D	D	D	D	D	D	D	D	D	D	D	D	D	D	D	D	0	16	0	9

[a] R–Republican, D–Democrat, E–Even. Hawaii and Alaska not included.

* Includes Progressives.

Table 4–7. Republican Party Dominance in Congressional Districts Won by the Same Party

Time Period	Total Number of Districts Won by the Same Party	Total Number of Districts Always Won by Republicans
1914–1926	270	148 (54.8%)
1932–1940	304	74 (24.3%)
1942–1950	322	147 (45.7%)
1952–1960	340	136 (40.0%)

By this measure of interparty competition, two conclusions stand out: (1) the number of congressional districts won by the same party over and over again is increasing; and (2) the Republican Party's share of these "no change" districts continues to be low. The trend toward recovery by Republicans during the 1940's did not continue during the 1950's. On the basis of these statistics alone, it seems that the congressional Republicans might conclude it is better for their electoral chances to have a Democrat in the White House than a Republican.

State and local election results repeat the general pattern that has been established by examining presidential and congressional results. Republicans do well in gubernatorial and state legislative races in those states that appear in Tables 4–4 and 4–6 as strong Republican states, though, as was true for national races, many formerly rock-ribbed Republican states have elected Democrats in recent years. The three most Republican states in sending Republican delegations to the House of Representatives—North Dakota, New Hampshire, and Vermont—all elected Democratic governors in 1962 and 1964.

Summary

When one studies the elections themselves, it becomes obvious that the cards are stacked against the minority party. The Democrats are the majority party and this means simply that they are preferred by a majority of the voters. The result is that the minority party must plan with extreme care just to maintain the *status quo* at election time. If the Democrats make a mistake in office, a Republican may win. If the Republicans select an attractive candidate and the Democrats an unattractive candidate, the Republicans may win. If the Republicans are better organized, spend more money, select the right candidates, turn out their voters, they may win. But the advantage is on the side of the party that is preferred by a majority of the voters. If they are equally effective, then the Republicans cannot win control of the national government.

Part II

The Republican Party and Policy-Making

CHAPTER 5

Republicans in Congress

PARTY ACTION IN ELECTIONS is relatively obvious, if not as yet adequately described. Party action in policy-making is not so obvious and descriptions of it are, for the most part, superficial. Some political parties texts do not devote any chapters to "party in government." Those that do, devote only one or two chapters out of perhaps fifteen to the subject. This is not a criticism of the authors of these texts. They would include more description of party action in policy-making if it were possible to do so. Unfortunately students of Congress have spent relatively little research time on the topic. In fact, the only efforts to study congressional parties since Paul Hasbrouck's *Party Government in the House of Representatives,* published in 1927,[1] have focused on roll calls—usually the last stage of the legislative process—or on possible reforms that would strengthen the party role in Congress (even though that party role has not yet been fully described and analyzed).

V. O. Key, Jr., offered one reason for the greater emphasis on party action in elections: "The high visibility of party activity in campaigns screens the fact that there are two radically different kinds of politics: the politics of getting into office and the politics of governing."[2] Others justify the lack of emphasis on congressional parties by pointing out that these parties are weak and ineffective.[3] As Austin Ranney and Willmoore Kendall observe:

> The parties *as such* . . . appear to have much less to do with determining what laws are passed and what administrative and judicial policies their appointees follow after they are installed in their respective posts. For example, party cohesion is usually weaker, and party affiliation a less powerful vote-influencing factor, in the Congress of the United States than in the legislatures of most of the world's other democracies; and certainly the parties' impact on congressional voting behavior and presidential-congressional relations is far more modest than most advocates of responsible party government and presidential leadership think it should be. And party influence is even less evident in the determination of national administrative and judicial decisions.[4]

---

[1] (New York: Macmillan, 1927).

[2] V. O. Key, Jr., *Politics, Parties, and Pressure Groups* (5th ed.; New York: Crowell, 1964), p. 653.

[3] Austin Ranney and Willmoore Kendall, *Democracy and the American Party System* (New York: Harcourt, Brace & World, 1956), pp. 397–399.

[4] *Ibid.,* pp. 407–408.

The basis for measuring party effectiveness has often been "the legislatures of the world's other democracies." The House of Commons in Great Britain is typically used as a basis for comparison. Regrettably, very few scholars treat congressional parties within the context of the political environment in which they act. One investigable question is: Given the political context within which American political parties must act, what is their function? Admittedly this question is of a different sort than that which asks about how our system rates with the British, but it is an important question. It is important for understanding the role of parties in policy-making and it is important if one wishes eventually to reform the party system. Effective reform can only take place if the actual changes are contextually appropriate—that is, are in line with the political context within which the object of reform is operating.[5]

What is the political context within which congressional parties operate? A principal feature is that of diffusion of power. The framers thought that it was important to divide power and they demonstrated great skill in institutionalizing their values. Federalism, separation of powers, frequent and staggered elections, bicameralism —these characterize the political context of congressional parties. This diffusion of power makes it extremely difficult for political parties to organize as centrally directed policy-making units. It is generally agreed, however, that parties have the responsibility of bridging the gaps created by the founding fathers. The majority party in particular is expected to bring order to institutional processes for solving public problems. The responsibility of the minority party is less clear, though most commentators agree that the minority should offer constructive criticism of the actions of the majority party. Neither party, however, can adequately meet the demands of the critics in fulfilling these responsibilities because of the nature of the constitutional system.[6]

Both parties have certain functions that are related to the goals of Congress. If we assume that the function of Congress in the political system is to resolve public problems, then political parties serve as major instrumentalities for facilitating communication in Congress. I

[5] In this connection, see Leon D. Epstein, "A Comparative Study of Canadian Parties," *American Political Science Review*, Vol. XVIII (March, 1964), pp. 45–59.

[6] Frank Sorauf in *Political Parties in the American System* (Boston: Little, Brown, 1964), p. 11, makes the valid point that ". . . the dispute over 'party responsibility' is in reality a dispute over the *kind of democracy we are to have*." [our italics]

stated earlier (see Chapter I) that political parties function to organize the policy-making process. In Congress, this organizational function is primarily a communications function. Parties organize legislators so that when policy problems are identified and solutions suggested, there will be mechanisms for communicating such information among party members, and strategies for implementing one solution over another can then be developed.

The above suggests that party is not primarily a decision-making unit for policy-making. That is, it is not within party *qua* party that public problems are acted upon. This is not to say that party actions have no effect on public policy. Party actions facilitate resolving policy problems—principally by providing mechanisms for defining problems, suggesting and winnowing solutions, and communicating agreed-upon strategies to members. But party itself is not the principal arena for initiating, developing, and ratifying policy actions.

Thus there are at least two major functions of congressional parties: first, the function in the political system to bridge the gaps created by the constitutional diffusion of power—the party's "political" function, which is performed principally by the majority party; second, the function in the legislative system to provide an organization that will facilitate communication in order that Congress might act to solve public problems—the party's "legislative" function. There is a third function—the party's "survival" function. Congressional parties perform certain activities that are essential for their survival. That is, in organizing to achieve the first two functions mentioned above, the party distributes rewards and incentives among its membership. This function is particularly important for the minority party because Congress becomes the refuge—the center of action in government—for the second party. Party leadership in policy-making for the Republican Party has been in Congress for all but eight years since 1932. If the party is to survive there must be, at the national level, some rewards for service—some incentive for Republicans to continue offering constructive criticism and facilitating communication.

The "legislative" and "survival" functions will be of principal interest here. The House Republican Party organization seems to function primarily to facilitate communication, whereas the Senate Republican Party organization seems to function primarily to offer rewards and incentives. There is less need for a formal party organization to facilitate communication in the Senate.

There are a number of variables which help to explain why congressional parties organize and function as they do at any one particular time. I have already referred to the differences due to majority-minority status in Congress. Other factors of importance include the characteristics of the legislative body—for example, the differences between the House and the Senate as legislative bodies are significant in determining the type of party organization that results. And, of course, the relationships between the legislative party and institutions outside the Congress help to determine how party organizes and functions in Congress. Thus, for example, one may expect that the Republican Party in Congress will function differently if a Republican rather than a Democrat is in the White House. Or, if there is a particularly active National Committee Chairman, such as the late Paul Butler for the Democrats, his activities may be a factor in determining how the congressional party operates. In each of the several possible sets of circumstances, one would expect that the congressional party will maximize those agencies, procedures, and organizational characteristics that are consistent with the functions it performs and minimize those that are not.

Republican Party Organization in the House

There is a real need for party organization in the House—more so than in the Senate. Consequently, the formal organizational structure of the House Republican Party is more critical for achieving the "legislative" function of organizing Republicans for purposes of communication than is its counterpart in the Senate. David Truman discusses reasons for the differences.

> Fundamentally these differences are traceable to the greater size of the House. In a body four and one-half times as large as the Senate . . . the individual member is scarcely visible to the electorate . . . a representative in contrast to a senator, is more likely to be perceived as one member of a party than as a name and a person in his own right.
> A member of the House, in short, is almost certainly more dependent than a senator. His dependencies may be many, but one of them is the party, and especially the legislative party.[7]

Even in 1937, when the Republicans had fewer House seats than any minority party since 1890 (and the House had only a total of 333 members in 1890), there were nearly as many in the House Re-

[7] David Truman, *The Congressional Party: A Case Study* (New York: Wiley, 1959), p. 194.

publican Party (89) as there were in the whole United States Senate (96). In recent years the number of House Republicans has averaged about 180. Thus there is always a need for a party organization to facilitate communication in the House.

Though the principal function of legislative party organization is that of facilitating communication, there are certain tasks that must be performed before that function can be realized. First, Republicans have to be elected to the House of Representatives. The legislative party and its leadership have an obvious interest in electing Republicans to the House. A special party campaign committee—the National Republican Congressional Committee—is set up for this purpose. (It has been described in Chapter II.) Second, it is necessary to assign House Republicans to the various standing committees, in essence, to give them work assignments when they get to Washington. Since 1911, a "committee-on-committees" has existed to assign Republicans to standing committees.[8]

The House Republican Committee-on-Committees is composed of one Republican—often the senior Republican—from each state having Republican representation in the House.[9] Thus, in 1964, West Virginia, with 1 Republican and 4 Democrats, had one representative on the Committee and New York, with 21 Republicans and 20 Democrats, also had just 1 representative. This disparity in representation is compensated for by allowing each member on the Committee to cast as many votes as there are Republican Congressmen from his state. Therefore, in 1964, the West Virginia member could cast only 1 vote; the New York representative could cast 21 votes. The large state delegations can, if they are able to agree among themselves, control the Committee. In any event, however, representatives from California (15 Republicans in 1964), Illinois (12), Michigan (11), New Jersey (8), New York (21), Ohio (18), and Pennsylvania (14), will naturally have considerable power in the Committee.

In 1964, there were 37 members of the Committee-on-Committees

[8] The only modern treatment of committee assignments in the House is that by Nicholas Masters, "House Committee Assignments," *American Political Science Review,* Vol. LV (June, 1961), pp. 345–357. Reprinted in Robert L. Peabody and Nelson W. Polsby, eds., *New Perspectives on the House of Representatives* (Chicago: Rand McNally, 1963), pp. 33–58.

[9] The House Democrats rely on the Democratic members of the House Ways and Means Committee, together with the Speaker and Majority Floor Leader, as their Committee-on-Committees. Members of Ways and Means are selected by the Democratic caucus. See Nicholas Masters, *American Political Science Review,* Vol. LV (June, 1961), pp. 346–348.

(13 states elected only Democrats to the House in 1962), plus the Chairman, Minority Leader Charles A. Halleck (Indiana). Since this is a rather unwieldy group and since certain large states have a majority of votes anyway, a Subcommittee is appointed by the Minority Leader. As Nicholas Masters pointed out in his study of committee assignments: "The Subcommittee receives and considers *all* applications for assignment and transfer, and the full Committee invariably accepts all of its recommendations."[10] Of course, it should be noted that not all House Republicans are assigned a committee at the beginning of each session. Only freshmen members and more senior members requesting transfer from one committee to another are assigned. The procedure is that the member makes his requests to the Committee-on-Committees, giving his first, second, and third choices. The Committee then checks with the ranking Republican on the standing committee that has a vacancy with respect to his preferences among the applicants. The ranking member's preferences are honored to the extent of not assigning a member to his committee whom he does not want. It is in this assignment procedure, of course, that party regularity becomes an important factor. Those who often "wander off the reservation" cannot hope for a major standing committee assignment.

Other party agencies in the House are more directly related to the functions of facilitating communication and dispensing rewards. These include party leaders and two major party groups: the Conference and the Policy Committee.

The Party Conference

Party organization at every level is composed of three basic party units—a mass meeting that theoretically is the font of authority for other units, committees, and leaders. In the national party organization, the mass meeting is the National Convention. In the House Republican Party organization, the mass meeting is called the "Conference." All House Republicans are members of the Conference.

The Conference (or caucus as it is sometimes called) has waxed and waned in influence. George Galloway describes the party caucus as being important in early Congresses and in the period immediately following the decline in the Speaker's power—1911 to the 1920's.[11]

---

[10] Masters, p. 349.
[11] George Galloway, *History of the House of Representatives* (New York: Crowell, 1961), Ch. 9.

When it was truly a center of authority, the majority's caucus performed a number of tasks: selection of party leadership and the Committee-on-Committees, approval of committee assignments, consideration of proposed amendments to House rules and legislative policy, and discussion of Capitol Hill patronage.[12] Though the Conference has by no means been the most powerful unit in the House Republican Party in recent years, it does have important functions and is a more significant unit than the House Democratic Caucus.

Galloway noted that the Conference met more than forty times during the Eisenhower Administration—about five or six times a year on the average.[13] The Conference has met even more often since 1961—as many as ten and twelve times a year. Normally, the most important meeting of the Conference is its initial meeting of a new Congress. A first order of business is the election of a Conference Chairman and Secretary. This election is usually uncontested but in 1963, as is described below, it was an occasion for an internal party struggle. The Conference then proceeds to the selection of various party leaders. A candidate for Speaker is nominated. He will become Speaker if the Republicans have a majority in the House; otherwise he becomes Minority Leader. The Policy Committee Chairman is elected and the composition of the Committee-on-Committees is approved (actual membership is selected by each state delegation). The Conference does not select the Whip. By Conference resolution, the Committee-on-Committees has that power.

The Conference may also consider changes in party organization in its initial meeting of a new Congress. For example, in 1949, the steering committee was disbanded and a policy committee organized. In 1959, the positions of Minority Leader and Policy Committee Chairman were separated. Finally, the Conference in its first meeting may take a stand on impending changes in House rules.

Other meetings during the year are called to consider party stands on legislation, to publicize Republican principles, or to hear reports from party committees. The Policy Committee may wish to submit an action it takes on legislation to the Conference so as to increase party unity on the measure. Of course, the Conference has the power to reject or alter any action taken by the Policy Committee, though it does not do so in practice.

The Republican Party Conference may, if it chooses, establish sub-

12 *Ibid.*, p. 141.
13 *Ibid.*, p. 155.

committees to study party problems and make recommendations. A recent example of such a group is the Subcommittee on Increased Minority Staffing, chaired by Fred Schwengel (Iowa). This Subcommittee has conducted research on the amount of staff for the minority on the standing committees and has pressed for increases.

All in all, the Republican Conference is an active caucus, particularly when compared to that of the House Democrats. Several of the junior members in the House Republican Party have expressed an interest in making the Conference even more active. They would like to see it better organized—perhaps with a number of specialized subject matter committees on major public problems—so that it might act as an organ to respond to the Democrats with greater force. These members had such reform notions in mind in 1963 when they organized a movement to oust Charles B. Hoeven (Iowa) from his position as Conference Chairman (though capturing a leadership position, not reform, was the principal motivation for the move). Hoeven had been Conference Chairman since 1957, when he took over in an orderly transfer from the retired Clifford Hope of Kansas. The insurgents in 1963, led by Charles E. Goodell (New York) and Robert P. Griffin (Michigan), were anxious to demonstrate dissatisfaction with House Republican leadership. They relied on the support of the large number of freshmen and sophomore members of the House Republican Party. After careful consideration, they calculated that their best chance for success was to mount a campaign to defeat Hoeven. Their candidate was Gerald R. Ford, Jr. (Michigan). Ford won by an 8-vote margin in a spirited Conference session, January 8, 1963. In addition to this victory, the group was successful in getting increased representation and voting strength on the Policy Committee. Goodell explained to his constituents, in a remarkably frank newsletter, what the insurgents had in mind.

> We wanted eight new members on the Policy Committee to represent the newer Congressmen. We wanted our Republican Conference to become a more imaginative instrument of policy. We were tired of finding our party in Congress too frequently cowering defensively in a corner when we felt we were completely right on an issue. We needed a shake-up in the leadership with some new blood at the top. We felt Charlie Halleck, the Minority Leader, would be strengthened, and our party strengthened, if we handled things the right way. We frankly wanted to shake the foundations a little bit without creating a permanent rift in our ranks.[14]

[14] Charles E. Goodell, M.C., Letter to Constituents, January 23, 1963.

Thus, though there are obvious problems with respect to a mass meeting ever being the real center of power, it is clear that the Republican Conference in the House has increased in stature. And there is every indication that this trend will continue under Chairman Ford. The Republicans can at present afford to rely on the Conference. They are, in general, less divided on most policy problems than are House Democrats. It would be expected that Democrats would maximize other techniques to facilitate communication so that they can contribute to unified action in Congress.

The Policy Committee[15]

During the congressional reform period in the 1940's one of the many reform proposals was to create policy committees in both houses of Congress. There was a policy committee provision in the Legislative Reorganization Bill of 1946, when it was approved by the Senate, but the House deleted it because Speaker Sam Rayburn opposed policy committees. The Senate later passed legislation authorizing policy committees, the House has not done so to this day.

When the Eighty-first Congress convened in 1949, House Republicans were disgruntled over the loss of 75 seats in the 1948 election. Moderates demanded some changes in party organization. They thought that the Republican record in Congress was not being effectively publicized by party leadership and asked that a policy committee be created to replace the steering committee—a party leadership group which had been moribund for years. Minority Leader Joseph W. Martin, Jr., agreed to the idea. He introduced a resolution in the party Conference to disband the steering committee and create a policy committee to advise House Republican leadership. Martin became Chairman of the newly formed Policy Committee, and he promptly relegated it to the status of the disbanded steering committee. As one House Republican summarized in an interview:

> Periodically Martin would call a meeting, but they were just bull sessions. Joe would get some sort of an idea of the way the wind was blowing but nothing more.[16]

---

[15] For a more extensive treatment of the House Republican Policy Committee, see Charles O. Jones, *Party and Policy-Making: The House Republican Policy Committee* (New Brunswick, N.J.: Rutgers University Press, 1965).

[16] Jones, p. 27.

In 1959, Martin was defeated by Charles A. Halleck for the minority leadership post. Part of the junior members' price for supporting Halleck in that fight was a guarantee that the Policy Committee would be revitalized under a separate chairman. John W. Byrnes (Wisconsin) was selected as chairman. The Policy Committee began to assume a significant role in the House Republican Party after 1959.

The Policy Committee membership is now composed of the party leadership (Floor Leader, Chairman and Secretary of the Conference, the Whip, and the Chairman of the Congressional Campaign Committee), the five Republican members of the Committee on Rules, members from various geographical regions, members-at-large, and representatives from the five most recent "classes" or "clubs" (that is, Eighty-fourth to Eighty-eighth Congresses).[17]

The regional representatives are elected by regional groups, which were established in the original Resolution. Each of nine regions has 1 representative for each 20 Republican Congressmen or fractions thereof. That is, all regions get at least 1 representative and if a region has over 20 Congressmen, it may elect 2 representatives to the Policy Committee. The Committee-on-Committees elects the members-at-large. Each "class" or "club" also receives representation based on the number of Congressmen in the group (for example, there were 31 members in the Eighty-eighth Congressional Club and therefore they elected two representatives to the Policy Committee). In 1964, there were 36 Policy Committee members, including the Chairman.

The Policy Committee has two major functions: research on major policy problems and development of policy stands on legislation. The research is conducted under the direction of a Subcommittee on Special Projects. John J. Rhodes (Arizona) is, at the time of this writing, Chairman. The research itself is done by a small staff. Since the Policy Committee has no official status in the House, there are no funds appropriated for staff, office space, or supplies. Thus, several Congressmen contribute to the Policy Committee from their own staff allocations.

Policy stands are developed in Policy Committee meetings. The Committee usually meets on Tuesday of each week that Congress

---

[17] Each group of Congressmen who are first elected at the same time form a "club." Thus, there is an Eighty-eighth Congressional Club made up of those Republican Congressmen elected for the first time in 1962.

is in session. There is discussion of pending legislation, usually led by Republican members of the standing committee which considered the legislation, and, if deemed appropriate, a definite position is taken. Normally, all House Republicans are sent a notice of the action taken so that they can vote accordingly, though no Republican is bound to support a Policy Committee stand.

Of course, the Policy Committee does not take a stand on all major legislation. If there is considerable division among Republicans on a particular bill, the Committee will not issue a party position notice. As one member noted: "We can't have minority reports from the Policy Committee." Thus, the Committee seeks to discover a basis for consensus on legislation; if none is to be found, it cannot take overt action.

All in all, the House Republican Policy Committee has developed into an active party unit in the last five years. It is not nearly as effective as many House Republicans would like it to be, but it is perhaps the most active and effective policy committee on Capitol Hill. The House Democrats, for reasons already noted, have no policy committee and their steering committee does not meet.

Party Leadership

As in most legislative party organizations, there are four principal routes to leadership: One may be elected to a leadership post; one may assume a leadership position because of length of service; one may capitalize on his expertise; or one may have a widely recognized personal capacity for leadership. There is, of course, no guarantee that any of these will actually result in the exercise of leadership. Elected leaders may only be "puppets," senior members may be inept, experts may be ignored, able leaders may be stifled by the system.

In the House Republican Party, there are three party leaders who are elected by the Party Conference and two who are elected by other bodies. The Conference elects its own Chairman (see above), the Minority Floor Leader (or Speaker and Majority Leader if the party is in the Majority), and the Chairman of the Policy Committee (see above). The Committee-on-Committees, which is chaired by the Minority Floor Leader, selects the Whip, and the Congressional Campaign Committee selects its own Chairman and other officials.

The Floor Leader is the party's procedural leader (see Table 5–1 for a list of Republican floor leaders in this century). His responsibilities require that he know the details of parliamentary procedure, the work schedule of the House, his own party's priorities on legislation, what Republicans have done in standing committees on legislation, what Republicans want to have done on legislation, what the Democrats are doing on legislation. In short, he must be a center of communication, a veritable "switchboard" through which flows information about everything that is going on in the House of Representatives. He devotes full time to these responsibilities and therefore is not a member of a standing committee. Though he has an interest in and must know about legislation when it is in the committee stage, his more active direction of Republican activity on bills begins when they are placed on the House calendars. Of course, the Minority Floor Leader, by definition, does not have a majority. His "direction" of legislation on the House floor is quite different from that of the Majority Floor Leader. If he is to have any victories on the House floor—whether these be in the form of passing Republican-sponsored legislation, amending or defeating Democratic-sponsored legislation, or recommitting bills to the standing committees—he must fashion a majority by getting Democratic votes and maintaining cohesion in his own party. Halleck has demonstrated considerable ability in capitalizing on Democratic Party division by keeping his forces united and thus negotiating occasional Republican victories.

The Minority Leader has a number of sanctions that can be brought to bear on his party members. He is chairman of the Committee-on-Committees. Party mavericks may find that their requests for transfer to other committees are denied. The Minority Leader has close working relationships with all ranking minority members of standing committees and with other party leaders. The recalcitrant party member may find that his legislation is bottled up, that he receives poor subcommittee assignments, that he has little time for questioning of witnesses appearing before his standing committee, has problems in scheduling his bills, that his requests for travel are denied, and the like. The Minority Leader also has a number of favors he can dispense. Appointments to special boards and commissions, space allocations, invitations—these and other special favors go to the party regulars, not to those who stray.

It is a fact that most minority party victories in the House and Senate will be of the negative sort—that is, defeating majority party

Table 5–1. Republican Party Leaders, House of Representatives, 1901–1964

Congress	Speaker	Floor Leader	Whip	Conference Chairman
57th	David Henderson, Iowa	Sereno Payne,* New York	James Tawney, Minn.	Joseph Cannon, Ill.
58th	Joseph Cannon, Ill.	"*	"	William Hepburn, Iowa
59th	"	"*	James Watson, Ind.	"
60th	"	"*	"	"
61st	"	"*	John Dwight, New York	Frank Currier, N.H.
62nd	—	James Mann, Ill.	"	"
63rd	—	"	Charles Burke, S.D.	William Greene, Mass.
64th	—	"	Charles Hamilton, New York	"
65th	—	"	"	"
66th	Frederick Gillett, Mass.	Franklin Mondell,* Wyo.	Harold Knutson, Minn.	Horace Towner, Iowa
67th	"	"*	"	"
68th	"	Nicholas Longworth,* Ohio	Albert Vestal, Ind.	Sydney Anderson, Minn.

Table 5–1. (continued)

Congress	Speaker	Floor Leader	Whip	Conference Chairman
69th	Nicholas Longworth, Ohio	John Q. Tilson,* Conn.	Albert Vestal, Ind.	Willis Hawley, Ore.
70th	"	" *	"	"
71st	"	" *	"	"
72nd	—	Bertrand Snell, New York	Carl Bachmann, W. Va.	"
73rd	—	"	Harry Englebright, Calif.	Robert Luce, Mass.
74th	—	"	"	Frederick Lehlbach, N.J.
75th	—	"	"	Roy Woodruff, Mich.
76th	—	Joseph Martin, Mass.	"	"
77th	—	"	"	"
78th	—	"	Leslie Arends, Ill.	"
79th	—	"	"	"
80th	Joseph Martin, Mass.	Charles Halleck,* Ind.	"	"

Table 5-1. (continued)

Congress	Speaker	Floor Leader	Whip	Conference Chairman
81st[a]	—	Joseph Martin, Mass.	"	"
82nd	—	Joseph Martin, Mass.	"	Clifford Hope, Kans.
83rd	Joseph Martin, Mass.	Charles Halleck,* Ind.	"	"
84th	—	Joseph Martin, Mass.	"	"
85th	—	"	"	Charles Hoeven, Iowa
86th	—	Charles Halleck, Ind.	"	"
87th	—	"	"	"
88th	—	"	"	Gerald Ford, Mich.

[a] In 1949 the House Republican Policy Committee was formed. There have been two chairmen — Joseph Martin, Mass., 1949–1959; John Byrnes, Wisc., 1959–present.

Sources: George Galloway, *History of the House of Representatives* (New York: Thomas Y. Crowell, 1961); *Congressional Quarterly Almanacs; Congressional Record;* Randall Ripley, "The Party Whip Organizations in the United States House of Representatives" *American Political Science Review,* Vol. LVIII (September, 1964), pp 561-576.

* Indicates Majority Floor Leader.

— Indicates a Democratic Speaker.

legislation. The reasons are simple. The minority may be expected to *oppose* majority party legislation, either in favor of their own alternative or in favor of doing nothing at all. Thus, when the majority divides on its own legislation, the negative votes of the majority and those of the minority will carry the day. It is much less likely that blocs of the majority and the minority will actually work together to propose bills. The party and the congressional committee system are not structured in this way. On the other hand, such cooperation is not unheard of. For example, the civil rights legislation in 1963–1964 was the result of a bipartisan effort by northern Democrats and northern Republicans. In such cases, the Minority Floor Leader takes an active role in the passage of the legislation.

As noted above, the Minority Floor Leader is elected in the Party Conference. Normally this selection is very much a routine matter of simple confirmation of the incumbent leader. There are exceptions, however. In 1919, when the Republicans had regained their majority position in the House of Representatives, Frederick Gillett of Massachusetts waged a spirited campaign against the incumbent party leader, James Mann of Illinois, and won, thus becoming Speaker of the House. Mann had been Minority Floor Leader since 1911.

A more spectacular overthrow occurred in 1959. Joseph W. Martin, Jr., was first elected to lead the Republican Party in the House of Representatives in 1939. The next year, Sam Rayburn was elected Speaker and for twenty years the team of Rayburn and Martin led the House. On two occasions they switched positions. In 1947–1948 and 1953–1954, Martin became Speaker and Rayburn Minority Floor Leader. When Martin was Speaker, he supported Charles A. Halleck, Indiana, for Majority Floor Leader. When the Republicans lost control of the House in 1948 and 1954, Halleck lost his leadership assignment in the party, though he continued to attend the leadership conferences at the White House during the Eisenhower Administration.

In the last days of Martin's reign, the tempo of criticism of his leadership increased. Junior members in particular were upset. They did not think there was adequate communication between themselves and the party leadership. They were concerned that Martin was not physically able to meet the demands of leadership. After several years of dissatisfaction, the younger members decided to act.

Congressional Republicans met disaster at the polls in 1958. When the Eighty-sixth Congress convened in 1959, there were 47 fewer Republicans in the House of Representatives. Many House Republicans agreed that the time was right for ousting Martin. Those leading the effort wanted one of their own group to replace Martin. A poll of their supporters showed that John Byrnes (Wisconsin) had the greatest support, followed by Gerald Ford (Michigan), and Charles Halleck. Halleck refused to withdraw from the race, however, and thus there was the possibility that Martin would win against a divided opposition. The insurgents marshaled their forces behind Halleck as the only possible candidate who could defeat Martin. Martin was seemingly confident of victory—an indication of the extent to which he had lost touch with his own party.

There were three ballots taken in the party Conference. On the first vote, the Conference agreed to a secret ballot procedure. This unusual procedure was favored by the Halleck forces, since many House Republicans did not want to vote openly against Martin. Then came the votes on party leadership. On the first ballot, Halleck got 73 votes, Martin 72, and there was 1 spoiled ballot. Because of closeness of the vote, a second ballot was taken. Halleck won, 74 to 70. For the first time in twenty years, House Republicans had a new leader. An embittered Joe Martin stepped down to join the rank and file.[18]

By Conference resolution the Republican Whip is selected by the Committee-on-Committees (see Table 5–1 for a list of Republican Whips in this century). Since this group is chaired by the Minority Floor Leader and the Whip is one of his principal assistants, the Floor Leader's preferences are certainly honored. The present Whip, Leslie C. Arends, Illinois, has held that post since 1944. It is his responsibility to keep members informed about the legislative program, conduct polls of party members to determine probable party strength on a vote, round up members to vote, particularly on roll-call votes, and act as an Assistant Floor Leader. The Whip is empowered to establish a communications network in the party to assist him in carrying out his responsibilities. In the Eighty-eighth Congress, Arends was assisted by a Deputy Whip (Charles B. Hoeven, Iowa), three Regional Whips (eastern, midwestern, and western-southern regions), and twelve Assistant Whips.[19]

As noted earlier, other House Republicans become leaders because

[18] For further details on the fight for Republican Party leadership, see Charles O. Jones, *Party and Policy-Making: The House Republican Policy Committee* (New Brunswick, N.J.: Rutgers University Press, 1965), Ch. 2; see also Joseph Martin, Jr., *My First Fifty Years in Politics* (New York: McGraw-Hill, 1960).

[19] See Randall Ripley, "The Party Whip Organizations in the United States House of Reprsentatives," *American Political Science Review*, Vol. LVIII (September, 1964), pp. 561–576.

they have been in the House for a long time or because they are expert in a substantive policy area or in House procedure. Certainly one must count Clarence J. Brown (Ohio) as a leader in the House Republican Party. He has been in Congress since 1939 and is the ranking Republican on the Committee on Rules. And in the area of economic policy, one would include Thomas B. Curtis (Missouri) as a party leader; in the area of civil rights, one would include John V. Lindsay (New York), though he had been serving only his third term in 1964. Obviously it is much more difficult to identify actual leaders by relying on the criteria of seniority and expertise. For example, one cannot be certain that the ranking Republican on standing committees will actually be the party leader on that committee. It seemed clear than John Byrnes (Wisconsin) was his party's leader on the Ways and Means Committee when Noah Mason (Illinois) was actually the ranking member. And the same was true of Charles Hoeven (Iowa) when William Hill (Colorado) was ranking Republican on the Committee on Agriculture. The fact is that too little is known about party leadership in the House of Representatives, so that we can only guess as to who are the real leaders.

David Truman studied the voting agreement on roll calls among seniority leaders—that is, committee chairmen and ranking minority members—and elected party leaders in the Eighty-first Congress. His findings show differences between the majority and minority parties. For the majority Democrats, there was a tendency toward agreement between the Floor Leader and the committee chairmen, especially concerning measures reported out by the chairmen's committees. There was less agreement between Republican Floor Leaders in the House and Senate and their ranking committee members. No doubt, as Truman indicates, this difference is owing in large measure to the fact that the Democrats had leadership from the White House and therefore had a definite program which the party sought to enact.[20]

In summary, the House Republican Party as contrasted with the Senate Republican Party must of necessity establish effective instruments for communicating. The party is too large for any one man to know all that is going on. As contrasted with the House Democratic Party, there is the possibility of relying on such agencies as the Policy Committee and the Conference because of the greater homo-

[20] David Truman, *The Congressional Party: A Case Study* (New York: Wiley, 1959), Chs. 4, 6, 8.

geneity among Republicans, and the *need* to do so because of the fact that victory can only come if Republicans are unified enough to capitalize on occasional Democratic Party defections.

Republican Party Organization in the Senate

In 1964, there were more members on the House Republican Policy Committee than there were Republicans in the United States Senate (36 as compared with 33), and yet there were Senate counterparts for ·all of the House Republican Party organizational units. It is less clear in the Senate what the function of party organization is. As in the House, party organization facilitates communication but because of the Senate's smaller size, the communication problem is less acute. The Conference can be used as a Policy Committee because there are so few members. Bases of consensus, if they exist, are more easily discovered, although not any more easily developed than they are in the House.

On the other hand, there is a need among Senate Republicans to offer rewards for service and to provide mechanisms to insure unity. The majority party controls the legislative program and the White House. Their leadership can provide any number of rewards to party members. The minority is not in the same position. In a sense they have to create rewards within the party by providing a multiplicity of leadership posts. Incidentally, of course, greater unity may be achieved by putting recalcitrant members on the "team" as leaders.

Thus, whereas the House party organization functions principally to facilitate communication, the Senate party organization functions principally to offer rewards, incentives and accolades to the more "individualistic" Senators. The "survival" function is more important than it is in the House.

Donald R. Matthews notes that the Senate Republican Party is "more formalized, institutionalized, and decentralized"[21] as compared to the Senate Democratic Party. "Every Republican a leader" seems to be the policy of the Senate Republicans. Nearly one fourth of the Republican Senators hold some position of leadership (8 of 33). The principal positions are those of Floor Leader, Whip, Chairman of the Conference, Policy Committee Chairman, Campaign Committee Chairman, and Committee-on-Committees' Chairman. There

21 Donald R. Matthews, *U. S. Senators and Their World* (Chapel Hill, N.C.: University of North Carolina Press, 1960), p. 124.

are also separate chairmen of the Calendar and Personnel Committees. There are so many party committees that in 1964 all Republican Senators, even the freshmen, served on at least one committee. Many served on more than one.

The Campaign Committee has a function similar to that in the House—that is, to get Republicans elected to the Senate. It is appointed by the Chairman of the Conference. In 1964, the Campaign Committee consisted of 10 members and was chaired by Thruston B. Morton, Kentucky.

The Committee-on-Committees assigns Senators to standing committees. The Committee, consisting of 11 members in 1964, is appointed by the Conference Chairman, subject to confirmation by the Conference. The Committee then meets to assign incoming Senators and those who wish to change committee assignments. Its recommendations are then submitted to the Conference for *pro forma* approval. In the House the Chairman of the Committee-on-Committees is the Floor Leader. In the Senate, there is a separate Chairman (Frank Carlson, Kansas, in 1964), but Professor Matthews notes that he "gains little influence from his party post because of the party's strict adherence to the seniority rule."[22]

The other party organs serve more directly to facilitate communication. The Party Conference is composed of all Republican Senators. Its duties are similar to those of the Conference in the House, although it meets more often (weekly during the Eisenhower Administration) and its chairman has more power (for example, he appoints members to the Campaign Committee, the Committee-on-Committees, and the Policy Committee). Before 1944, the Floor Leader served as Conference Chairman. Since that time the posts have been held by separate men (see Table 5–2). There is discussion of pending legislation in the Conference, but actions of that body are not binding on the members; indeed, votes are rarely taken to indicate formally what the consensus is. The Chairman of the Conference in 1964 was Leverett Saltonstall (Massachusetts); the Secretary was Milton Young (North Dakota).

Both Democratic and Republican Policy Committees in the Senate are official in the sense that they are authorized by law and therefore receive congressional appropriations. After the provision for these committees was deleted from the Legislative Reorganization Bill of 1946, the Senate authorized policy committees for itself by attaching

[22] Matthews, p. 125.

an item to the Legislative Branch Appropriation Act in 1947. George Galloway notes that the committees were to "plan the legislative program, coordinate and guide committee activity, focus party leadership, and strengthen party responsibility and accountability."[23] These are lofty and important goals, but there is very little evidence that either of the two committees approach them. Both Hugh A. Bone and Malcolm E. Jewell agree that the exact function of the Committee depends on who is Chairman and whether there is a Republican in the White House.[24] Taft, according to Jewell, was a strong Chairman —so much so that he overshadowed Kenneth Wherry, the Floor Leader.[25] Successors to that position have not been so powerful. If there is a Republican in the White House, the center of Republican policy-making is bound to be there, rather than in the Senate.

The exact composition of the Senate Republican Policy Committee has changed over the years. Generally it has been a small committee —10 to 14 members. In 1956, however, all those Senators who were up for reelection (a total of 23) were appointed to the Policy Committee in order to add to their prestige. Presently, there are 14 members. All of the party leaders are members—the Floor Leader, the Whip, the Chairman, and the Secretary of the Conference, and the chairmen of the Campaign Committee, Committee-on-Committees, and Personnel Committee. Six additional members are appointed by the Conference Chairman, subject to the approval of the Conference. The Chairman of the Policy Committee (Bourke B. Hickenlooper (Iowa), in 1964) is elected by the Conference.

The Senate Policy Committee is served by a relatively large staff, generally over 15 persons. This staff also serves the Republican Conference. Principally the staff is engaged in research, publicity, and assisting Republican Senators with speeches, bill drafting, and any number of other services that the Senators request.

It is generally agreed that the Republican Policy Committee is more active than the Democratic Policy Committee. It is, as Hugh Bone describes it, "more institutionalized and publicized."[26] This

23 George Galloway, *The Legislative Process in Congress* (New York: Crowell, 1955), p. 335.

24 Hugh A. Bone, "An Introduction to the Senate Policy Committees," *American Political Science Review,* Vol. 50 (June, 1956), pp. 339-359; Malcolm E. Jewell, "The Senate Republican Policy Committee and Foreign Policy," *Western Political Quarterly,* Vol. 12 (December, 1959), pp. 966–980.

25 Jewell, *Western Political Quarterly,* Vol. 12 (December, 1959), p. 85.

26 Hugh A. Bone, *Party Committees and National Politics* (Seattle, Wash.: University of Washington Press, 1958), p. 195.

greater activity should not lead one to believe that the Committee performs more effectively than do the other policy committees in terms of the goals intended by those who first proposed policy committees. As in the House, the Senate Policy Committee does not *make* policy. Nor does it even discover the bases of consensus on policy—not because it cannot, but rather because it is not necessary for it to do so. When there are only 33 Senators, a leader can very quickly get the sense of the group; it isn't necessary for him to call a meeting of the Policy Committee. If he is not certain as to what his colleagues are thinking, he can just as easily call a Conference. Thus, the Policy Committee serves principally to provide additional staff aid to Republican Senators and for the purpose of discussing legislative scheduling. One might well question whether such committees are really necessary in the Senate at present. I do not think the same thing could be said for the House, which, interestingly enough, does not authorize such committees.

Republican Party leadership in the Senate, like that in the House, is composed of those elected to their posts, those who develop seniority, those who are expert in a subject area, and those who have recognized leadership ability. Once again, however, it must be reiterated that the smaller size of the Senate Republican Party means that there is a completely different pattern of communication and leadership. The Minority Floor Leader may well see and talk with most of his members every day. Furthermore, though he must know details of parliamentary procedure, he can be more of a substantive leader than can his counterpart in the House. Procedure is less formal, less impersonal in the Senate. The Minority Floor Leader may take the lead in introducing substantive amendments to legislation for his party, whereas a "substantive expert" from a standing committee would probably exercise that responsibility in the House. The Senate Minority Leader retains membership on standing committees; the House Minority Leader does not. All of this does not mean, of course, that the Floor Leader in the Senate is more effective in achieving party unity than is his counterpart in the House. In fact, Senator Dirksen may have more difficulty than Congressman Halleck simply because House Republicans individually have less power than do Senate Republicans and must depend more on party leadership.

Table 5–2 lists Senate Republican leaders during this century. It is interesting to note that during the early Congresses, Fifty-seventh through Sixty-second, the majority floor leadership post was held by several different men—three during the Fifty-eighth Congress. George H. Haynes, in his history of the Senate, emphasizes the importance of personal, unofficial leadership in the Senate. During the period 1901–1911, Senator Nelson Aldrich, Rhode Island, was the principal leader in the Senate, though he served as Floor Leader only during the Sixtieth Congress.[27] Apparently the floor leadership post was not the position of influence that it is today. Haynes notes that the Republicans relied on the seniority rule in electing the floor leader. It seems that the position of Floor Leader is still in the process of development.

Some functions of the Whip are the same as those in the House (See Table 5–2 for a list of Whips in this century). That is, he is responsible for insuring that Senators are aware of impending votes, or quorum calls, and that they are aware of a party position, if there is one. In addition, however, the Senate Republican Whip, Thomas H. Kuchel (California) in 1964, seems to be relied on more as a Deputy Floor Leader than is true of the House Republican Whip. Again, this difference is probably directly related to the difference in size. The House Whip has a sizable responsibility in getting Republicans to the floor for key votes. Senator Kuchel has very little problem in contacting all of his members.

House and Senate Leadership Conference

It has long been the hope of congressional reformers that there might be more coordination and cooperation between the party leaders of the two houses and between Congress and the President. The provision for policy committees, as originally passed by the Senate, included a section which provided for a "Joint Legislative-Executive Council." This Council would be composed of the majority policy committees of the two houses, meeting with the Executive. The whole proposal was deleted in the House.

At one time, just after the formation of the House Republican Policy Committee, there were joint meetings of the Senate and House groups. Hugh A. Bone records that the meetings were discontinued because of poor attendance by House members.[28] Republican party

---

[27] George H. Haynes, *The Senate of the United States* (Boston: Houghton Mifflin, 1938), Vol. 1, pp. 489–492.
[28] Hugh A. Bone, *Party Committees and National Politics* (Seattle, Wash.: University of Washington Press, 1958), p. 176.

Table 5–2. Republican Party Leaders, Senate, 1901–1964

Congress	President Pro Tempore	Floor Leader	Whip[a]	Conference Chairman[b]
57th	William Frye, Me.	Eugene Hale, Me.* Orville Platt, Conn.*		
58th	"	George Hoar, Mass.* Eugene Hale, Me.* William Allison, Ia.*		
59th	"	William Allison, Ia.* Eugene Hale, Me.*		
60th	"	William Allison, Ia.* Nelson Aldrich, R.I.*		
61st	"	Eugene Hale, Me.* Shelby Cullom, Ill.*		
62nd	"[c]	Jacob Gallinger, N.H.* Shelby Cullom, Ill.*		Shelby Cullom, Ill.
63rd	—	Jacob Gallinger, N.H.		Jacob Gallinger, N.H.
64th	—	"	James Wadsworth, N.Y. Charles Curtis, Kans.	"
65th	—	"	"	"
66th	Albert Cummings, Ia.	Henry Lodge, Mass.*	"	Henry Lodge, Mass.
67th	"	"*	"	"

Table 5–2. (continued)

Congress	President Pro Tempore	Floor Leader	Whip[a]	Conference Chairman[b]
68th	"	"*	"	"
69th	Albert Cummings, Ia. George Moses, N.H.	Charles Curtis, Kans.*	Wesley Jones, Wash.	Charles Curtis, Kans.
70th	"	"*	"	"
71st	"	James Watson, Ind.*	Simeon Fess, Ohio	James Watson, Ind.
72nd	"	"*	"	"
73rd	—	Charles McNary, Ore.	Felix Hebert, R.I.	Charles McNary, Ore.
74th	—	"	d	"
75th	—	"	d	"
76th	—	"	d	"
77th	—	"	d	"
78th	—	Wallace White, Me.	Kenneth Wherry, Neb.	"
79th	—	"	"	Arthur Vandenberg, Mich.
80th[e]	Arthur Vandenberg, Mich.	Wallace White, Me.*	Kenneth Wherry, Neb.	Eugene Millikin, Colo.
81st	—	Kenneth Wherry, Neb.	Leverett Saltonstall, Mass.	"

Table 5–2. (continued)

Congress	President Pro Tempore	Floor Leader	Whip[a]	Conference Chairman[b]
82nd	—	Styles Bridges, N.H.	"	"
83rd	Styles Bridges, N.H.	Robert Taft, Ohio* William Knowland,* Calif.	Leverett Saltonstall, Mass.	Eugene Millikin, Colo.
84th	—	"	"	"
85th	—	"	Everett Dirksen, Ill.	"
86th	—	Everett Dirksen, Ill.	Thomas Kuchel, Calif.	Leverett Saltonstall, Mass.
87th	—	"	"	"
88th	—	"	"	"

Sources: *Senate Manual;* Senate Republican Policy Committee; Senate Library.

* Indicates Majority Floor Leader.

— Indicates a Democratic President Pro Tempore.

[a] Whips were first elected in 1915.

[b] Data not available prior to 1911.

[c] Several Senators served as President Pro Tempore during this Congress.

[d] No Whip was selected during these years, though the Floor Leader could appoint Senators to assist him when necessary. Apparently McNary did appoint Warren Austin, Vermont, and Wallace White, Maine, as assistant leaders between 1940 and 1944, when Whips were again elected.

[e] The Senate Republican Policy Committee was created in 1947. Its Chairmen have been: Robert Taft, Ohio, 1947–1953; William Knowland, Calif., 1953; Homer Ferguson, Mich., 1953–1954; Styles Bridges, N.H., 1955–1962; Bourke Hickenlooper, Ia., 1962–+.

leaders of the two houses, however, have traditionally had meetings. When Eisenhower was President, they met with him at the White House. Now they apparently meet regularly to discuss strategy, usually every week. Those attending are the Floor Leaders, Whips, Conference Chairmen, Policy Committee Chairmen, ranking Republican on the Rules Committee, and perhaps others who are invited to attend.

Then there is the famed "Ev and Charlie Show," which was inaugurated to counterbalance the press and television attention given to President Kennedy. The two Floor Leaders met regularly with the press for the purpose of clarifying congressional Republican positions and attacking the Democratic Administration. Although the "Show" has by no means gained as much attention as had President Kennedy, it has received considerable publicity—not all of it favorable. Some Republican Congressmen opposed the press conferences, suggesting that substantive experts from standing committees should present views on specific legislation, not "Ev and Charlie." As one summarized it in an interview:

When Ike was in, the policy was stated by him or one of his representatives or Halleck. We now have what the press calls the "Ev and Charlie Show." I don't think it is a serious problem but we now have a lot of young members and these young Turks think that the image of the party would be better if, let's say, Bob Griffin [Michigan] spoke on labor and Al Quie [Minnesota] on agriculture. They think about the image projection.[29]

Party Unity in Congress

The discovery that British parties are more cohesive in voting in Parliament than are American parties in Congress has been cause for concern among many political scientists.[30] It has been charged that our parties are not responsible, and any number of corrective

29 Charles O. Jones, *Party and Policy-Making: The House Republican Policy Committee* (New Brunswick, N.J.: Rutgers University Press, 1965), p. 114.

30 A. Lawrence Lowell was the first to demonstrate this difference between British and American parties in his study, "The Influence of Party Upon Legislation in England and America," *Annual Report of the American Historical Association for 1901* (2 vols.; Washington, D.C., 1902), I, pp. 321–544.

measures have been suggested.[31] In general, the criticism that congressional parties are not cohesive enough has not been complemented with an analysis of the conditions that cause American parties to be less cohesive in voting than British parties. I have alluded to some of these conditioning factors in the early part of this chapter.

In recent years, there have been a number of roll-call studies that have been less concerned with how much party cohesion there should be than with how much cohesion there actually is. These works have attempted to identify other groups in Congress that might possibly rank higher than political party on measures of cohesion. Perhaps the most renowned of these studies is that by Julius Turner, *Party and Constituency: Pressures on Congress.* Turner examined metropolitan and rural pressures, foreign and native pressures, sectionalism, and party, and concluded that ". . . in spite of the small degree of party voting in the modern American Congress compared with other countries and other times, party continues to be more closely associated with congressional voting behavior than any other discernible factor."[32]

A more intensive study of party and roll-call voting was conducted by David B. Truman. Truman studied one Congress—the Eighty-first. One of his "threads" of evidence was that there is ". . . a clear tendency toward partisanship in both House and Senate that distinguished most members of the majority parties from most of those in the minority."[33]

There are those who continue to argue with such conclusions. They have in mind a legislative body wherein all Republicans vote together on a party policy that has been hammered out in party caucuses. If the description of the political context within which congressional parties act is accurate, then one would not expect to achieve perfect party cohesion, or anywhere near it.

How unified is the Republican Party in Congress? Since 1949 the Congressional Quarterly Service has compiled "party unity" scores

---

[31] Note in particular: Committee on Political Parties, American Political Science Association, "Toward a More Responsible Two-Party System," *American Political Science Review,* Vol. XLIV (September, 1950, Supplement); the recent work by James MacGregor Burns, *The Deadlock of Democracy: Four Party Politics in America* (Englewood Cliffs, N.J.: Prentice-Hall, 1962); Senator Joseph Clark, *Congress: The Sapless Branch* (New York: Harper, 1964).

[32] (Baltimore, Md.: Johns Hopkins University Press, 1951), p. 34.

[33] David B. Truman, *The Congressional Party: A Case Study* (New York: Wiley, 1959), p. 280.

for all Congressmen and Senators. Party unity roll calls are those in which the majority of one party vote against the majority of the other party. Generally about 45 per cent to 50 per cent of all roll calls are of this type. Party unity scores for individual members are based on the percentage of party unity roll calls on which a member votes in agreement with the majority of his party. Generally speaking, the average scores for the House and Senate Republicans tend to be higher than for the Democrats, but the differences, are not great. The overall average party unity score for Senate Republicans, 1949–1963, was 73.6; for the Democrats, 72.5. The overall average party unity score for House Republicans, 1949–1963, was 75.3; for the Democrats, 74.0.[34]

Party unity scores differ, depending on the substance of the legislation that is the subject of the roll call. Truman found that Senate Republicans were more unified on civil rights and internal security, labor, and public power issues and were less united on agriculture, foreign policy, and public works issues. House Republicans were more unified on issues such as civil rights and internal security, labor, housing, taxation, and general appropriation cuts and less united on issues such as foreign aid, agriculture, public works, veterans, and economic controls.[35]

Summary

In a constitutional system which so efficiently distributes power among various institutions, the political party is expected to coordinate action—to bridge the gaps created by federalism, separation of powers, bicameralism. Its success in this assignment is limited, for obvious reasons.[36] Congressional parties organize to facilitate communication in order that public problems will be solved. The majority party assumes the major responsibility for solving these problems; the minority party assumes the responsibility for criticizing and offering alternatives. Congressional parties also seek to maintain themselves— to survive. In the case of the House Republican Party, an effort is

[34] In 1955, the Congressional Quarterly Service changed its procedure for calculating party unity scores with the result that scores after that time are lower.

[35] Truman, pp. 51, 149.

[36] Some people argue that parties maintain the division, that parties do not centralize power but perpetuate its diffusion. The argument here is not that parties centralize power, but that they act as links between various power centers so that some coordinated action is possible.

made to maximize those agencies that do facilitate communication so that the opposition can be effective. Increasing reliance is placed on the Policy Committee and the Conference. The House Democratic Party can learn too much by such communication—so much that they are impeded in accomplishing their responsibility on policy-making. They prefer other means of communicating.

In the case of the Senate Republican Party, there is less need for formal means of communication. On the other hand, there is, I think, greater need than in the House, for offering rewards in the form of party positions to Senators. This greater need stems from the naturally greater individualism of Senators and the fact that in recent years, notably since 1958, there have been so few Republican Senators that there might well be a sense of frustration for the party overall in performing those functions expected of it.

CHAPTER 6

A Republican in the White House

PROFESSOR Clinton Rossiter, in his book *The American Presidency,* lists "Chief of Party" as one of the President's many roles. "No matter how fondly or how often we may long for a President who is above the heat of political strife, we must acknowledge resolutely his right and duty to be the leader of his party."[1] Part of every working day in the White House is devoted to party matters in some form.

In the past thirty-two years, Republicans have not often had the luxury of knowing who precisely was their "chief of party." During twenty-four of those years, there was a Democrat in the White House and whereas that party could be assured of the identity of its top leader, the Republicans never really knew. The search for the center of decision-making in the minority party becomes a sort of game. The National Committee Chairman, the defeated presidential candidate, congressional party leaders, former Presidents, all are mentioned at some point. The game is bound to end in frustration, however, because the fact is that there is no single decision-making center for the minority party.

Such are the ironies and realities of American politics that when the Republican Party did get a definite leader, he came "out of the blue." For the patterned mind, it would not have been incongruous in 1952 if "Mr. Republican," Robert A. Taft, had been the candidate, had been elected and thus assumed the role of "Chief of the Republican Party." Indeed, even Eisenhower said in his recent book *Mandate for Change* that Taft had "every right to think of himself as the logical candidate of the Republican Party."[2] Taft, however, did not become the leader. Republicans bestowed this honor on an Army general whose Republican affiliation was not known until 1952.

Why did the Republican Party choose as its leader a man with no party record? In large part, that question can be answered by under-

---

[1] Clinton Rossiter, *The American Presidency* (2nd ed.; New York: Harcourt, Brace & World, 1960), p. 31.

[2] Dwight D. Eisenhower, *Mandate for Change* (Garden City, N.Y.: Doubleday, 1963), p. 44.

standing something about the party and its frustrations, the man and his personality, and this nation and its politics. After twenty long years, many Republicans were beginning to doubt that they would ever see the inside of the White House again. The results of the 1948 election had been a major disaster—not merely an upset. In 1952, Republicans wanted a winner. Though Taft led early in the battle for Convention votes, the Eisenhower forces began to slice into his lead by parlaying their own candidate's personal popularity and the slogan "Taft can't win" into victory at the Convention.

General Eisenhower's effect on the American people is not easily described. He was a "dream" candidate. Though a war hero who commanded the combined armed forces on "D-Day," June 6, 1944, he did not fit the usual image of an Army general. Thus, he was able to combine the advantage gained from his being a symbol of victory over Adolf Hitler with an almost unbelievably warm and winning personality. Good old "Ike" was tough when the chips were down— when America had to be defended—but he was a man of peace, a gentle person, a man with a smile that could melt the heart of a Democrat. The slogan for the campaign became "I Like Ike" and very few Americans could deny it.

Thus the Republican Party turned away a man who had been labeled "Mr. Republican"—a man who had devoted his life to public service through partisan Republican politics—and selected a "winner." After twenty years, the temptation was too great; the taste of victory had too long been denied the party. One can understand a good bit about American politics by understanding how a professional could be defeated by an amateur in 1952.

The significance of the party's decision to choose Eisenhower rather than Taft will be debated for a long time. There is no definite answer. The topic for this chapter is not what might have been but what was the relationship between the first Republican President in twenty years and the Republican Party. As has been emphasized throughout, the Republican Party is the minority party. This fact will be of paramount importance in describing Eisenhower's relations with his party.

Before describing Eisenhower as "chief of party," it should be noted that it is no easy task to isolate the President's party role from other roles he plays. His major responsibility is clearly the constitutional responsibility he has as Chief Executive. His performance, of course, has party implications since, if he is successful, he will likely be reelected. Even if he is retiring, however, a successful President is of more value to the party than an unsuccessful President. Thus, in one sense, everything that the President does has an effect on his political party. In general, the President is more likely to be identified as playing the party role when dealing with Congress and with his own party organization. The President's dealings with congressional parties is more policy-oriented. He attempts to develop reliable liaison with and leadership in the congressional Republican parties. Usually this firm relationship with the congressional parties is for a *public policy* purpose—that is, in order that the President's program for taking action on public problems will be effected. In negotiating with his own party leadership in Congress, however, he might well deal in the type of political currency we normally identify as partisan politics.

His dealings with the extragovernmental party organization—at national, state, and local levels—is likely to be election-oriented. Like it or not, and Presidents vary in how much they like this responsibility, every man in the White House gets involved in party organizational problems, including such unpleasantries as party finance, intraparty conflicts over leadership, and recruitment and endorsement of candidates. There is incentive for the President to be involved, since (1) he may be seeking reelection and will need a strong party organization; (2) he wants his party to control Congress so that his program will have a better chance of passage; and (3) as a party man, he wants to use the White House to strengthen his party throughout the nation so that Republicans will continue to be elected after he retires.

Eisenhower and Congressional Republicans

President Eisenhower first faced the Congress on February 2, 1953, as he delivered his State of the Union message. His party was able to organize both houses by slim margins—an 8-vote majority in the House and 48–47 split in the Senate. Wayne Morse (Oregon) was the 96th Senator—he had just left the Republican Party to become an Independent. As Eisenhower looked out over his first Congress, he no doubt thought about the fact that none of his party leaders— Joseph W. Martin, Jr., and Charles A. Halleck in the House, Robert A. Taft and Leverett Saltonstall in the Senate—had ever served as congressional party leaders under a Republican President. Their experience as leaders had been as opponents to Democratic Presidents. Indeed, of these leaders only Martin had ever served as a member of Congress under a Republican President. Of the 221

House Republicans, only 15 had served under a Republican President. Of the 48 Senate Republicans, none had served under a Republican President. The senior Republican Senator, Styles Bridges of New Hampshire, was first elected in 1936. Congressional Republicans were used to opposing the Executive. Few of them had had very much training in cooperation.[3]

It could be hypothesized that it never takes a majority long to act like a majority, regardless of their previous experience. This hypothesis could not be tested in the congressional Republican parties during the Eisenhower years. In two short years House and Senate Republicans found themselves in their familiar minority role. It is a fact of profound significance in understanding congressional Republicans' view of their relationship with Eisenhower that whereas he continued to triumph, they continued to lose at the polls. Not even the President's sweeping victory in 1956 was sufficient to elect a majority of Republicans to Congress. Between 1954 and 1960, the Republican Party suffered from conflicting demands and expectations. It was the majority party in the White House, the minority party in Congress and the nation. House and Senate Republican Party leaders were charged with the responsibility of enacting the President's program while opposing congressional Democratic leadership. Meanwhile President Eisenhower was forced to work with congressional Democratic party leaders, for without their cooperation, his programs would be defeated.

Eisenhower did not like partisanship. There is no doubt that much of his success as a candidate and as President was owing to the fact that he was "above politics." In this regard, Eisenhower was, as Richard Neustadt has pointed out, *sui generis*.[4] Certainly Eisenhower differed from his immediate predecessor, Harry S. Truman, in the extent of his interest in partisan politics. To President Truman, Republicans were the enemy. Eisenhower had not experienced the type of political training that would lead him to regard all Democrats as the enemy.

[3] Eisenhower mentions the "unfamiliarity" of Republicans with the "need of cooperating with the Executive," in *Mandate for Change* (Garden City, N.Y.: Doubleday, 1963), p. 192.

[4] Richard Neustadt, *Presidential Power* (New York: Wiley, 1960), p. 194. See also Eisenhower, Chs. 1 and 2, for his discussion of his entry into politics; and Herbert Hyman and Paul Sheatsley, "The Political Appeal of President Eisenhower," *Public Opinion Quarterly*, Vol. 19 (1955–1956), pp. 29–39. Reprinted in Nelson W. Polsby, *et al.*, eds., *Politics and Social Life* (Boston: Houghton Mifflin, 1963).

Further, Eisenhower was the party's first winner in twenty years. And much of his campaign was pitched in an "above politics" tone. The result was, as Richard Rovere so congently observes, that "Truman's party put Truman in power; *Eisenhower put Eisenhower's party in power*."[5] [our italics] The President's victory was fashioned by the votes of Republicans, Independents, and *Democrats*. As has been emphasized before, Eisenhower could only win if some Democrats would vote for him. They did. His overwhelming victories made him President of all the people.

These factors—the minority status of congressional Republicans, Eisenhower's lack of partisan training, and the nature of his victories —are important in explaining his attitude toward Congress and congressional parties. Emmet John Hughes discusses Eisenhower's relationships with Congress in his book *The Ordeal of Power*. Hughes pronounces as false the notions that Eisenhower was too lazy to lead Congress, or that he lacked interest, or was intimidated by arch conservatives. Eisenhower was sensitive to this criticism and, according to Hughes, had a speech on the subject which included his conception of leadership:

> ". . . you do not *lead* by hitting people over the head. Any damn fool can do that, but it's usually called "assault"—not "leadership" . . . I'll tell you what leadership is, It's *persuasion*—and *conciliation*— and *education*—and *patience*. It's long, slow, tough work. That's the only kind of leadership I know—or believe in—or will practice."[6]

In his book on the early days of his Administration, Eisenhower describes how he dealt with Congress.[7] He established a congressional liaison office, headed by General Wilton B. Persons. Individuals with experience on Capitol Hill were appointed to assist General Persons. Weekly meetings with legislative leaders were held in the Cabinet Room of the White House. During the first two years of the Administration only Republican leaders attended; when the Democrats won control of Congress, their leaders also were invited. Eisenhower reports that he was disappointed in the lack of unanimity between himself and congressional leaders. "It was clear that habitual, almost instinctive opposition to the Chief Executive, as well as dif-

[5] Richard Rovere, *The Eisenhower Years* (New York: Farrar, Straus, 1956), p. 112.

[6] Emmet John Hughes, *The Ordeal of Power* (New York: Dell Publishing, 1964), p. 108.

[7] Eisenhower, Chs. 5, 8, 12.

ferences in political convictions, would create difficulties in Executive Legislative relations."[8]

One man who helped to build effective cooperation between the
two branches was Senator Robert A. Taft, Senate Majority Leader.
Eisenhower lauds Taft's leadership and willingness to lead the fight
for Administration programs. It seemed apparent that following
Taft's untimely death, July 31, 1953, President Eisenhower never
again had a leader on the Hill in whom he had so much confidence.

If Eisenhower believed in persuasion, conciliation, education, and
patience in working with Congress, he was never able to convince his
principal assistant, Sherman Adams, of the need to rely on such
techniques. Louis Koenig quotes Adams as saying that "I don't believe
there's a different set of rules for working with Congress than for
working with other people." Koenig then comments:

> He did, in fact, treat Congressmen no better or worse than he
> treated general mankind. The Governor [Adams], accordingly, growled
> and snapped and took healthy bites out of the pride of influential
> legislators just as he did with citizens of lesser station. Although some
> legislators, realizing the pressures Adams was under in his big job,
> were tolerant of his manner, his slights and rebukes prompted scores of
> Congressmen to turn against him.[9]

There is ample support for Koenig's conclusion in Adams' book
on the Eisenhower Administration.[10] Though he was once a member
of the House of Representatives himself, Adams has very little good
to say about Congress or congressional Republicans. When discussed
at all, they are treated as "problems," "difficulties."

One final item on Eisenhower's view of Congress. Eisenhower
often spoke of "modern Republicanism." He apparently was much
impressed with a book by Arthur Larson entitled *A Republican
Looks at His Party*.[11] According to Adams, the President considered this book a good summary of his own philosophy of government.[12] There is no doubt that many senior Republicans in Congress
did not fit the category "modern Republican."

[8] *Ibid.*, p. 195.

[9] Louis Koenig, *The Invisible Presidency* (New York: Holt, Rinehart &
Winston, 1960), p. 381.

[10] See Sherman Adams, *First-Hand Report* (New York: Harper, 1961).

[11] (New York: Harper, 1956).

[12] Adams quotes Eisenhower's response to a question in a press conference about Larson's views. "Eisenhower said that although he might not agree
with every word in Larson's treatise, 'he expressed my philosophy of government as well as I have seen it in a book of that size.' " (See p. 298, *First-
Hand Report.*)

How did congressional Republicans view the President? To begin with, senior congressional Republicans were not anxious to be told by the "elegant amateur"[13] what was and what was not "modern Republicanism." To the extent that there was a policy-making center for the Republican Party, it had been in Congress for twenty years. It was only natural that Congressmen would hesitate to follow a man who referred to them and their supporters as "these Republicans."[14] As Joe Martin observes, *"Republican* was a word that was not on the tip of his [Eisenhower's] tongue."[15]

The President's lack of partisan training was one cause for concern on Capitol Hill. There is an atmosphere of professional partisanship in Congresss. There are certain rules of the game and Eisenhower and Adams violated many of them. Joe Martin (who was at the time Republican leader of the House) recounts that to his horror he picked up a newspaper in his district and read that the Administration had appointed a lawyer from Wellesley, Massachusetts, as an Assistant Attorney General. "A man from my own district had been given this important federal post, and reading it in a local paper was the first I knew of it! What a way this was to go about strengthening the local Republican organization!"[16]

Republican members of the House were candid in discussing their frustrations under the Eisenhower Adminisration in interviews I conducted in 1962.[17] Senior members were upset because the White House became the center of decision-making. They had to accept the "direction flag from the White House"—becoming no more than a "handmaiden" of the Administration. Two members expressed themselves as follows:

> When Eisenhower was President all the leaders went to the White House in the morning to get his ideas. Then they came back and sold these ideas to the [House Republican] Policy Committee. We who were against the White House position had a hard time blocking action.

[13] Rossiter, p. 31.
[14] Richard Rovere, *The Eisenhower Years* (New York: Farrar, Straus, 1956), p. 112.
[15] Joseph Martin, Jr., *My First Fifty Years in Politics* (New York: McGraw-Hill, 1960), p. 223.
[16] *Ibid.,* p. 224.
[17] The interviews were conducted as part of a study of the House Republican Policy Committee, attempting to determine if the Policy Committee operated differently under Republican and Democratic Presidents. See Charles O. Jones, *Party and Policy-Making: The House Republican Policy Committee* (New Brunswick, N.J.: Rutgers University Press, 1965), Ch. 4.

Under Eisenhower it was a problem of whether to support him or not. Your criticism of the Administration had to be much more careful because it was a Republican Administration. You had to keep your mouth shut if you opposed. Of course, it is my philosophy that Congress is the government and that concept is in jeopardy now.[18]

When a Democrat was in the White House, these members were more comfortable. In referring to the Kennedy Administration, one member said, "It is more fun now." Another expressed the same notion:

> Now all we have to do is vote "no." I always said that when Truman was President, my job was easy. All I had to do was vote "no." During the Eisenhower Administration, Republicans had to accept a policy even though it was against their principles.[19]

To some members, there was even a troublesome legacy for having had a Republican in the White House. That is, they were committed to certain programs because of pressure from Eisenhower, and when John F. Kennedy became President, they were "stuck" with their own record. "Thus, there is a problem of distinction between Kennedy and Eisenhower—that is, *in finding where we can base our opposition*. This is the problem caused by the Eisenhower years."[20]

Senior members of the congressional party were frustrated because they had led the Republican Party for several years and were not anxious to accept leadership from President Eisenhower, a man whose political skills they doubted. Many junior members had other complaints. They were concerned that there was not enough liaison between themselves and Eisenhower. They were not objecting to leadership from the White House—indeed they welcomed it—but they thought they had something to contribute to the process of solving public problems and that Eisenhower should consult them. One such member expressed his ideas to Joe Martin in a letter, following the 1958 election.

> Let's start having a few bull sessions down at the White House on these issues, attended by the Congressmen who have been dealing in these areas for years. If the White House personnel mean what they say when they talk about a "team," let them start acting as team leaders. The first thing to do is to change the White House attitude toward Congressmen. Congressmen do know something, and some of them do

18 Jones, pp. 82–83.
19 *Ibid.*, p. 83.
20 *Ibid.*, p. 85.

work hard. Their ideas are worth listening to. For six years this Administration has not availed itself to any extent of ideas the Republican Congressmen might have given them about issues that have confronted this nation.... Instead of White House conferences with so-called "public spirited citizens" on issues of the day, let's have a few White House conferences with Republican Congressmen who, by their very job, are public-spirited citizens and, by their work, have had to deal practically with these problems over a period of many years.

... By and large, every time I have discussed matters of public interest with members of this Administration, I have come away with the feeling that I was listened to because they didn't want to antagonize a "politician" who might take it out on them in some "mean" political way. I felt I was not listened to as one who was really more interested in good government than they were ... more interested because I had made more sacrifice in my personal life by staying in politics and facing the people in election after election.[21]

One source of difficulty between these members and the White House was Sherman Adams. Adams stood between them and the President. Professor Koenig noted that "Adams considered it his high duty to keep people and their problems from the President. . . ."[22] This was Adams' "buffer" role. One House Republican gave an illustration of Adams as "buffer." Adams would not let the member see the President about an expenditure in the member's district that had been eliminated.

The greatest sense of frustration by Republicans during the Eisenhower years was in trying to get to Ike. He was too protected by Adams. I went to the White House for breakfast at the end of the week and when I saw Ike, I told him that I was angry about that [Adams' elimination of the expenditure]. He didn't know the funds had been cancelled but knew about the program. He called Adams over but by then the funds couldn't be restored. Kennedy now has ———— [Democratic Senator from his state] getting this legislation introduced and they will pass it and get credit for it. With Adams we [House Republicans] were almost suspect.[23]

In summary, the situation between 1952 and 1960 was such that one could hardly expect normal relations between congressional and presidential Republicans. A Republican was in the White House because he was not too identified with his party. Republican leadership in Congress included members strongly identified with their party. These leaders were given only two years to adjust from minority to majority status and were then returned to minority status.

[21] *Ibid.,* pp. 31–32.
[22] Koenig, p. 352.
[23] Jones, pp. 159–160.

Republican Support of the President's Program

Any President has a number of tools on which he can rely for gaining support for his program in Congress. The standard list of these tools is well known: patronage, veto, messages to Congress, control over sessions, press conferences, legislative liaison personnel, and conferences with party leaders. Professor Richard Neustadt has not been satisfied merely to list the tools in his inquiry into presidential power. He is interested in the "sources of presidential power" in making public policy. He identifies at least three:

> . . . first are the bargaining advantages inherent in his job with which to persuade other men that what he wants of them is what their own responsibilities require them to do. Second are the expectations of those other men regarding his ability and will to use the various advantages they think he has. Third are those men's estimates of how his public views him and of how their publics may view them if they do what he wants.[24]

Most of the "tools" fall in the first category—bargaining advantages inherent in the office itself. For Eisnehower, as with most Presidents, the veto and his control over information were particularly useful tools. Patronage was of less importance than for any previous turnover of administrations owing to the extension of civil service. Sherman Adams notes in his book that "the patronage pickings were so lean under Eisenhower that they became a subject of grim humor among the Republican politicians in Washington." At one leadership meeting, Senator Leverett Saltonstall (Massachusetts) asked Joseph Martin if he had been able to get any new jobs for constituents. Martin replied: "New jobs? I lost two that I got when Truman was in office."[25]

Eisenhower's greatest source of power was clearly his prestige outside Washington. Congressmen, bureaucrats, party officials, all were aware of his phenomenal popular support, and as a result, tried never to be put in a position of opposing Eisenhower. Neustadt, however, questions the extent to which Eisenhower capitalized on this or any other source of power. Compared to Roosevelt, Eisenhower's power sense was "blunt."

> As late as 1958 he had not quite got over "shocked surprise" that orders did not carry themselves out. Apparently he could not quite ab-

[24] Richard Neustadt, *Presidential Power* (New York: Wiley, 1960), p. 179.
[25] Adams, p. 61. Martin tells a different version of the same story in his book, p. 225.

sorb the notion that effective power had to be extracted out of other men's self-interest; neither did he quite absorb the notion that nobody else's interest could be wholly like his own. And he seems to have been unaware of all his natural advantages in turning different interests toward his own.[26]

Thus Neustadt raises some doubt that President Eisenhower would have behaved differently as a party leader, even if there had been a Republican Congress. His lack of political training and the nature of his victories, then, seemed more important factors in determining how he led than the fact that he had to work with a Democratic majority in Congress.

Since 1954 the Congressional Quarterly Service has compiled presidential support scores (based on roll-call votes on which the President had taken a stand) in an effort to determine the extent of congressional support for presidential programs. Table 6–1 presents the House and Senate scores for the two parties, 1954–1963. During the Eisenhower Administration, the Senate Republican Party was rather consistent in its support, ranging from a low of 66 per cent in 1960 (the last year of the Eisenhower Administration) to a high of 73 per cent (the second year of the Administration). The House Republican Party was less kind to the President, their scores ranging from 54 per cent in 1957 to 71 per cent in 1954. Democratic scores range from 38 per cent in 1954 to 56 per cent in 1955 in the Senate and 40 per cent in 1959 to 55 per cent in 1958 in the House.

Scores for the Kennedy Administration show an expected reversal, with the Democrats supporting and the Republicans opposing. When the scores for the two administrations are averaged (see Table 6–1), some interesting conclusions result.

During the Eisenhower years:
1. Senate Republicans supported Eisenhower more than did House Republicans. (70–63)
2. House Democrats supported Eisenhower more than did Senate Democrats. (48–44)
During the Kennedy Administration:
3. House Democrats supported Kennedy more than did Senate Democrats. (72–64)
4. Senate Republicans supported Kennedy more than did House Republicans. (40–37)
When comparing the two Administrations:
5. Senate Republicans supported Eisenhower more than Senate Democrats supported Kennedy. (70–64)

[26] Neustadt, pp. 163–164.

6. Senate Democrats supported Eisenhower more than Senate Republicans supported Kennedy. (44–40)

7. House Democrats supported Kennedy more than House Republicans supported Eisenhower. (72–63)

8. House Democrats supported Eisenhower more than House Republicans supported Kennedy. (48–37)

What does all of this say about presidential-congressional relations? All in all, it appears that the Senate Republicans are the greatest source of support for a Republican President. Note that their average is considerably higher than that of the House Republicans (conclusion 1). One might assume that this higher average is the result of the Senate generally offering greater support to a President, but Senate Republicans offered greater support to Eisenhower than did Senate Democrats to Kennedy (conclusion 5).

House Republicans are not so generous to a Chief Executive— even their own. Their support score was the lowest of any party group for its President. Note in particular that House Democrats gave considerably more support to Kennedy than House Republicans gave to Eisenhower (conclusion 7).

Table 6–1. Presidential Support Scores, 1954–1963

Year	Senate		House	
	Republicans	Democrats	Republicans	Democrats
1954	73	38	71	44
1955	72	56	60	53
1956	72	39	72	52
1957	69	51	54	49
1958	67	44	58	55
1959	72	38	68	40
1960	66	43	59	44
1961	36	65	37	73
1962	39	63	42	72
1963	44	63	32	72
Mean Support Scores				
1954–1960	40	64	37	72
1961–1963	70	44	63	48

Source: *Congressional Quarterly Almanacs.*

The situation is reversed on the Democratic side. The House Democrats offered the greatest support to their President (conclusion 3) and to the Republican President (conclusion 2).

One can only speculate about the reasons for these differences. The major variables probably include constituency differences, institutional differences, and differences in power structure and leadership. Thus, it may be that Republican Congressmen represent more conservative districts within a state, whereas the Republican Senator from the state is more liberal because he represents the entire state. Perhaps the reverse is true for the Democrats—that is, Democratic Congressmen represent the liberal areas within a state but the state is conservative all in all and this fact is reflected in senatorial representation. Or the differences may be a result of the fact that Senate Republican and House Democratic leadership is more effective in producing majorities for the President than is House Republican and Senate Democratic leadership. Or perhaps the differences are due to the kinds of men who are able to gain power in each of the congressional parties. Whatever the precise reasons for the differences, it is clear, on the basis of the data presented in Table 6–1, that a Republican President can depend more on Senate Republicans than on House Republicans. It is also evident that any President must take into account the differences between the Senate and House Republican parties in negotiating to enact his program.

Finally, it can be observed that congressional Republicans are less likely to support a President of the other party than are congressional Democrats (conclusions 6 and 8). Of course, this may be a result of the fact that the Democrats were the majority party in Congress during six of the eight years of the Eisenhower Administration and therefore accepted some responsibility for the President's program. Evidence for this interpretation appears in Table 6–1. Both House and Senate Democrats had relatively low scores in 1954, when the Republicans were still the majority party. In 1955, both scores exceeded 50 per cent (56 in the Senate, 53 in the House). The average support score during 1954–1958 for House Democrats was 52 per cent (compared to 48 overall) and for Senate Democrats, 47.5 per cent (compared to 44 overall). Both support scores drop during the last two years of the Eisenhower Administration, probably because of the impending 1960 election and the fact that congressional Democrats had a 2 to 1 majority in both houses and could make more demands of their own on policy.

Eisenhower and the National Republican Party

President Eisenhower was not fond of having to deal with congressional parties, but at least these negotiations were often directly related to policy outcomes. His "above politics" mentality dictated an intense dislike, however, for having to participate in the activities of the national party organizations. Their politics were "politics politics" and probably the kind he discussed in a press conference in 1955 when he said, "I have no great liking for that."[27]

Like it or not, however, there are demands and expectations which bring the President into the thick of national party politics. As Cotter and Hennessy note:

> There is no ambiguity of leadership in the party which has the presidency. The president is the leader. He may delegate his leadership responsibilities as he likes, but the ultimate responsibility is his, and he may claim and take full credit or blame for the party decisions which are made during his administration.[28]

In accepting the general thesis of this argument, it must be noted that President Eisenhower was more successful in avoiding this responsibility than any other President in modern times.

Eisenhower selected five national chairmen. Arthur Summerfield, Michigan, was first selected to head the National Committee during the 1952 campaign. He was then appointed Postmaster General and resigned as Chairman. The next appointee was C. Wesley Roberts from Kansas. He had hardly got used to the title when he was forced to resign owing to conflict of interest charge in his home state. Leonard Hall, New York, was then appointed and he held the post from 1953 through the 1956 election—an unusually long tenure for a Republican National Committee Chairman. H. Meade Alcorn, Connecticut, and Senator Thruston Morton, Kentucky, served out the last years of the Eisenhower Administration.

The national party organization was always *used* by Eisenhower, but seldom assisted by him. When he sought reelection in 1956, the President relied to a considerable extent on the organization. Cotter and Hennessy observe that only in 1956, of the three campaigns between 1952 and 1960, "have the RNC [Republican National Committee] staffers been in the front lines of the Republican cam-

---

[27] *New York Times,* June 1, 1955.
[28] Cornelius Cotter and Bernard C. Hennessy, *Politics Without Power: The National Party Committees* (New York: Atherton Press, 1964), p. 81.

paigns."[29] The National organization was used as an organization, however, and not an adviser. In his description of the 1956 election, Emmet Hughes makes it clear that the strategy of the campaign was developed in the White House, not in the Republican National Headquarters.[30] During the early days of the campaign, Eisenhower did not respond to the Democrats, who continued to fill the press with their campaign activities. ". . . this rather quickly began to disconcert and unnerve the Republican National Committee under Leonard Hall."[31] When he did speak up, Eisenhower emphasized the grave problems that continued to face the United States, rather than stressing that all was rosy under a Republican Administration. This focus, according to Hughes, dismayed many members of the National Committee.[32]

Eisenhower also used the organization between elections to handle patronage problems, party organizational problems, and to conduct congressional campaigns in 1954 and 1958. As a matter of fact, Leonard Hall can be described as one of the most influential and important of all the Republican National Chairmen—superlatives usually reserved for out-party chairmen. His position was enhanced by the fact that Eisenhower gave him responsibilities that other Presidents reserve for themselves. On the other hand, the President's distaste for patronage matters and other party organization matters was bound to make the party professionals feel like "second cousins." Leonard Hall was invited to Cabinet sessions when patronage matters were to be discussed. Emmet Hughes' description of these meetings is particularly revealing about (1) the President's view of national party organization problems and (2) the extent to which the National Chairman was aware of the President's view.

> Hall . . . always entered with the air of someone slightly astonished at being admitted, slightly fearful of peremptory dismissal. There was a nervous and hesitant tone to his appeals for "cooperation with the National Committee" in rewarding the political helpful with departmental posts. Squirming unhappily in his chair and perspiring profusely, he would half-implore, half-lecture his listeners. . . . "Our first job is to build the Republican party into a true majority party. This not only takes a program but real reorganization. . . . We haven't made *one* appointment that can directly help to win *one* Congressional seat in

29 Cotter and Hennessy, p. 125.
30 Emmet J. Hughes, *The Ordeal of Power* (New York: Dell Publishing, 1964), pp. 157–158.
31 Hughes, p. 157.
32 Hughes, p. 158.

1954. We haven't appointed a single Italo-American—or a single Polish American." Then—in the rushed and anxious voice of an advertising agency's account-executive talking against the clock in a sedate board of directors meeting—he tried to beguile the "business-like" Cabinet: "Now, I've got my own new team. They're no political hacks. With just one exception, they are all from business corporations. So we won't be recommending hacks to you." At last, desperately: "We want to be able in the future to rely on our own organization, not running for help to the President all the time. . . ." Some quality—or lack of it—in this appeal so exasperated the President that he would snap, as on this occasion: "Quit apologizing for what you're saying—and tell us what you want." And with such almost petulant expressions of distaste, Eisenhower tended almost always to show his contempt for the power of patronage.[33]

On the problems of conducting congressional campaigns, Professor Philip Wilder, who served on the Chairman's staff in 1958, describes the frustrations of Meade Alcorn in 1958. Most Cabinet members refused to participate in the campaign, and when Chairman Alcorn expressed doubt in public that the Republicans could carry the Senate, President Eisenhower chided him in a press conference by saying: "I don't know why he would say that. Now for my part I have never yet admitted defeat on any fight I had to fight."[34] For the most part, the 1958 congressional election was not a fight the President felt he had to fight—that was Chairman Alcorn's responsibility.

Summary

This chapter has focused on the question: What happens when the minority party wins the White House? The answer seems to be that the party is rather frustrated. Between 1952 and 1960, the Republican Party captured the White House with a "man on a white horse." Since the party was not able to win along with its candidate, it developed a touch of schizophrenia. It was a minority with a temporary majority for its presidential candidate. No one was quite certain how to act; there were conflicting expectations for all concerned.

It may well be that during these periods of one-party dominance, the minority party can only hope to win solid control of the Presidency and then only with a candidate who can attract voters from

[33] Hughes, p. 114.
[34] Philip Wilder, Jr., *Meade Alcorn and the 1958 Election* (New York: McGraw-Hill, 1959), p. 14.

both parties. It is very likely that a minority party President will have to face majority party control during part of his tenure in the White House. Thus, when a Republican is in the White House during a period of Democratic Party dominance, there will probably be a relatively high degree of bipartisanship. And, interestingly enough, it appears that having a Republican President does not help the minority party become the majority party. In fact, it may even be detrimental to minority party growth. Since a Republican President will probably have to work with congressional Democrats in order to enact his program, he will deemphasize partisanship except during presidential election years. As President Eisenhower observed:

> I have never enjoyed the luxury of being head of a majority party. Perhaps the leader of such a party can be uniformly partisan. But the leader of a minority party has a different set of references. To win, he and his associates must merit the support of hundreds of thousands of independents and members of the opposition party. Attitudes, speeches, programs, and techniques cannot be inflexibly partisan.[35]

On the other hand, the minority party must be fed with an occasional presidential victory if it is to have incentive to survive. Further, as my good friend, Professor Harold Rhodes, argues, the occasional victory for the minority party is necessary so that it will not become too negative in its criticism. It must have full responsibility for solving public problems periodically, or it cannot continue to offer criticism of the constructive or innovative type.

Such is the dilemma faced by the minority party, it seems. Winning the Presidency will not be particularly helpful to the party in its attempt to become the majority party; indeed, it may even hinder that development. Losing the Presidency over and over again may have even more deleterious effects.

---

[35] Eisenhower, p. 431.

CHAPTER 7

The Future of The Republican Party

IT IS INEVITABLE that any examination of a minority party will eventually lead the student to comment on prospects for the minority becoming the majority. Throughout I have suggested that there are many obstacles to any lasting shift in power between the two parties at the national level. Historically, political parties in the United States have had to assume semipermanent roles as majority and minority parties. There has not been frequent trading back and forth. The majority party stays the majority party; the minority party stays the minority party. When lasting changes have occurred, they have been the result of major domestic crises. Short-term shifts have resulted from less serious domestic crises, internal divisions in the majority party, and an attractive minority party presidential candidate winning over a less attractive majority party candidate.

Much of the foregoing discussion no doubt seems fatalistic to the reader. I have made reference to a number of factors that tend to prevent the Republican Party from becoming the dominant party—for example, the persistence of partisan attachment by citizens of voting age, the low level of issue awareness on the part of voters, the tendency to reelect congressional and senatorial incumbents, the political advantages that accrue to the majority party from their control of the machinery of government combined with the disadvantages suffered by the minority party in their not having research agencies available to develop policy alternatives, the greater attention given the majority party in the mass media, the likelihood that a minority party President will be hamstrung by having to work with a majority party Congress, and the lack of an effective, centralized party organization. These are only a few of the obstacles preventing the minority party from gaining control. They are formidable enough to make one fatalistic.

Still, the Republican Party has survived and is able to threaten most Democratic Party candidates. Is there a possibility that the Republican Party can do more than threaten? Short of a major domestic crisis, the Republican Party can become the majority party only by convincing more citizens to identify themselves as Republicans. Least likely to be convinced are those who already identify with the Democratic Party. Most susceptible are those who have not as yet formally or actively identified with the Democratic Party or who are experiencing some change in their lives that might lead them to change party identification.

Young people, those who are older but have not voted before, and those who classify themselves as independents, would fit into the first category. There is no guarantee, of course, that all of them will become Republicans even if approached. Young people tend to follow their family's partisan affiliation, and a majority of families identify with the Democratic Party. Nonvoters may well be apoliticals. Independents may sincerely wish not to identify. But there is a greater chance of strengthening the Republican Party by concentrating on these citizens than on those already formally committed. The second category of people mentioned above includes the many Americans who move from place to place—from the central city to suburbs and from one region or city to another. Again, there is no guarantee that if a Republican Party worker calls on these people to assist them in integrating into a new community, as one example of a contact, that they will identify with the party, but there is at least some chance that they will.

In order to convince more Americans to identify with the Republican Party two elements at minimum are essential: time and organization. Obviously it takes some time before large numbers of people can be convinced to identify with the Republican Party. Unfortunately, political professionals are not able to think in long-range terms. Most of their effort must be spent meeting short-term demands.

A strong national organization—one that can set organizational and tactical goals for the party overall and command the machinery for effecting the goals—is the second essential. As noted above, lack of an effective, centralized party organization is one of those factors that prevent the minority party from attaining majority status. The analyst might easily recognize the minority party's problems and prescribe solutions, but any solution requires a mechanism for implementation. The blunt fact is that American political parties, and, in particular, the minority party, do not have such a mechanism.

So, having recognized some of the problems and having suggested one logical solution, fatalism again rears its unwelcome head. Is there still no cause for hope among Republicans? While the national party organization is by no means an effective decision-making unit, capable of setting organizational goals and pursuing them, it has developed strength in the past twenty years. There is every indication that it will continue to grow. That growth does offer hope. I would argue that until the Republican national party organization does develop and is able to be a center of goal-setting and decision-making, it is highly unlikely that the party can plan to become the majority party. It may win the White House, and even the Congress for a short time, because of circumstantial conditions—for example, attractive candidates combined with mistakes made by the majority party. It may become the majority party because of a calamitous event. But these are factors which are, for the most part, not subject to control by the Republican Party.

I would never deny that there is some hope, however slim, that the Republican Party can plan to become the majority party in the immediate future. At the same time, I would argue that the weight of the evidence is not in its favor. And I should like the student of American parties to carry away from this analysis the realities of party politics in this country—not slim hopes based on misunderstanding. Even for the hopeful, however, there are lessons to be learned from hard facts which advise "how to succeed in minority party politics by trying very hard indeed." That is, the more that is understood (and faced) about the Republican Party's situation, the more likely it will be that Republicans can focus their efforts where they will have greatest effect.

Thus, barring a cataclysmic event, it is likely that the Republican Party will continue to function as the party of *criticism* in the immediate future. Let us forget for a moment the presumed desire of any party to be the majority party and comment on its role as critic. Is our second party able to criticize as effectively and constructively as it should? The answer to such a question depends on what one's values are. I value constructive criticism as part of an effective democratic political system, and I do not think that we maximize the advantages of criticism which might be gained from the minority party. In a world in which foreign and domestic policy problems are increasingly complex, the minority party does not have the equipment for making a detailed evaluation of majority party policy nor for offering policy alternatives.[1] Valiant efforts are made by the Republican Party to develop alternative solutions, but the fact is that the out-party lacks national leadership, centralized organization,

---

[1] Though not of immediate relevance, the same criticism might be, and has been, leveled at the party of *advocacy*—the majority party.

committee staff in Congress, other research facilities, and information about policy problems. If it is true that Americans value criticism and wish to institutionalize it, then we are not gaining full advantage from one major institution of criticism—the minority party.

Nostrums

Fortunately for the vitality of the American two-party system, Republican politicians are not fatalistic about their party's chances. Many of them would scoff at much of the analysis herein and continue to offer varieties of solutions designed to return the party to its "rightful" position as a majority party. At present, there are at least two and possibly three discernable groups within the party that offer prescriptions for success. In general, these groups can be classified along a left-right continuum. They differ both in principles the party should espouse, and the methods that should be employed to recapture the majority position.

The first group to consider is that led by former Senator Barry M. Goldwater of Arizona. It is the conservative, or right wing, of the party. The conservatives have long been denied dominance in the national party organization, though they traditionally have had strength in the congressional party. In recent years, the Republican National Convention has selected the more moderate over the more conservative presidential candidate. Senator Robert A. Taft came close to the nomination in 1952, but could not defeat his popular opponent. In 1964, however, the conservatives had their day. They were able to nominate their man. They were able to test their nostrum. The results were catastrophic for the Republican Party.

The essence of the remedy offered by the conservatives for the Republican Party is a mixture of a particular philosophy and a bipartisan, or more accurately, an extrapartisan organization which will attract all those who believe in that philosophy. Republicans in this group claim that victory has eluded the party because it has not been true to its own traditions; it has not been vocal enough in stating a philosophy; it has been a "me too" party. The conservative philosophy of these Republicans is outlined in a book by Goldwater, *The Conscience of a Conservative.*[2] The conservative is one who takes heed of the differences between men and therefore "makes pro-

2 (New York: Hillman Books, 1960.) See also his book *Why Not Victory?* (New York: McGraw-Hill, 1962.)

vision for developing the different potentialities of each man . . ."[3] Politics is the "art of achieving the maximum amount of freedom for individuals that is consistent with the maintenance of the social order."[4] In practical terms this philosophy means:

> I have little interest in streamlining government or in making it more efficient, for I mean to reduce its size. I do not undertake to promote welfare, for I propose to extend freedom. My aim is not to pass laws, but to repeal them. It is not to inaugurate new programs, but to cancel old ones that do violence to the Constitution, or that have failed in their purpose, or that impose on the people an unwarranted financial burden. I will not attempt to discover whether legislation is "needed" before I have first determined whether it is constitutionally permissible. And if I should later be attacked for neglecting my constituents' "interests," I shall reply that I was informed their main interest is liberty and that in that cause I am doing the very best I can.[5]

On the domestic scene, of course, there is an emphasis on "states rights." In foreign policy, there is an emphasis on victory in the cold war since "we can establish the domestic conditions for maximizing freedom . . . and yet become slaves. We can do this by losing the Cold War to the Soviet Union."[6]

If this philosophy can be projected to the American voter by an effective national and state party organization, the conservatives argue, then the Republican Party will win because a majority of Americans are conservative. But there is a need to revitalize some state organizations, build others, and coordinate their activities at the national level. No section of the country will be ignored, but principal emphasis will be placed on the South, Midwest and West. A truly conservative candidate will win the South, it is argued, and for the first time in history the Republican Party will be a national party, winning in all sections of the nation.

The second group in the Republican Party takes a different view of what the party should do. These are the "moderates," and they have had several leaders. The most recent is President Eisenhower. The moderates take quite a different view of the American voting public. A majority can be fashioned by projecting an image of the party as a moderate party because most Americans are moderate.

---

3 *The Conscience of a Conservative*, p. 11.
4 *The Conscience of a Conservative*, p. 13.
5 *The Conscience of a Conservative*, pp. 23–24.
6 *The Conscience of a Conservative*, p. 88.

The most coherent statement of moderate Republicanism is that by Arthur Larson, *A Republican Looks at His Party*.[7] Eisenhower is said to have endorsed this statement as an accurate reflection of his own philosophy. While endorsing the importance of the individual as "the pre-eminent object of all our political arrangements,"[8] Larson recognizes the need for government in society. "Whatever can be done privately should be done privately," and "Government should be as local as possible," but government does have certain responsibilities that it must accept. Among these responsibilities are maintaining prosperity, "enabling working people to improve their lot through fair collective bargaining," and providing for the general welfare of the people.[9]

Throughout Larson's book there is an emphasis on balance, consensus, merging. President Eisenhower, in Larson's view, "discovered and established the Authentic American Center in politics."[10] This New Republicanism fashioned by the President would prevail because it represents the vast majority of Americans. It, like the conservative solution, would be bipartisan in the beginning. Eventually, however, New Republicanism would be fighting the Opposition. The Opposition refers to "any doctrine, regardless of party affiliation of the person who asserts it, which is at odds with the American Consensus as here described."[11]

In order to coalesce the majority of moderates, an organization that is less partisan is necessary. Though not discussed in great detail in Larson's book,[12] Eisenhower and his associates have demonstrated by their actions what they think is necessary to achieve their goals. During 1952 and 1956, there was great reliance on organizations that were not directly associated with the Republican Party—for example, volunteer groups, Democrats for Eisenhower, Independents for Eisenhower. Even now, the former President is Honorary Chairman of a group called Republican Citizens Committee of the United States.

[7] Arthur Larson, *A Republican Looks at His Party* (New York: Harper, 1956). See also Eisenhower, *Mandate for Change* (Garden City, N.Y.: Doubleday, 1963), various chapters.
[8] Larson, p. 199.
[9] Larson, 200–202.
[10] Larson, p. 10.
[11] Larson, p. 11.
[12] Though Larson does note that there is no American Center Party and probably won't be. The traditional Republican Party is simply advised to capitalize on the existence of "the" consensus. See Larson, p. 16.

There is a third group that is somewhat less distinct. They are very close to the moderate position but they tend to be more liberal, especially on the issues of civil rights and urban problems. For the most part these are Republicans from highly industrialized and urban states. Many of them are in the United States Senate—for example, Jacob K. Javits, Clifford P. Case, Thomas H. Kuchel—but the most active national representative of the group has been Governor Nelson A. Rockefeller of New York. These men and their supporters are active in their opposition to the conservative philosophy and strategy. They reject any plan to win the South by adhering to a states-rights approach on civil rights. Senator Javits states the Liberal's position:

> The "Southern strategy" is ... at odds with the heritage and tradition of the Republican Party—the party of Union, the party of Lincoln, the party that wrote the civil-rights amendments into the Constitution, making the defense of Negro rights a national instead of a local matter.[13]

This third group also suggests a separate strategy for making the Republican Party a majority party. They would concentrate Republican efforts in the large metropolitan areas of the nation, attacking Democratic boss rule and trying to attract Democratic and independent votes by offering impressive alternative programs for solving public problems. Senator Javits emphasizes in his book *Order of Battle* the need for Republicans to recognize that "metropolitan man will comprise 80 per cent of the population by 1970."[14] Efforts should be made, Javits advises, to solve the problems of metropolitan man.

Thus there is very real division in the Republican Party as to how the party should proceed.[15] Each group is convinced of the reality of its analysis and the probability of success if it could but implement its remedies. They differ in philosophy and how that philosophy can·be parlayed into victory. But they agree on one thing: that victory will come only with an above-party emphasis. For the conservatives, it is a problem of collecting the majority of conservatives they know exists in the country. The moderates would make it the Center against

[13] "To Preserve the Two-Party System," *New York Times Magazine* (October 27, 1963).

[14] Jacob K. Javits, *Order of Battle: A Republican's Call to Reason* (New York: Atheneum, 1964), p. 313.

[15] For a much more detailed analysis of the party division, see Conrad Joyner, *The Republican Dilemma* (Tucson, Ariz.: University of Arizona Press, 1963).

the Opposition. The liberals would have it be the Progressive majority against those who would thwart progress. So it is with the minority party. Victory must be fashioned by attracting those outside the party.

If the Republican Party is to become the dominant party in America, however, those outside the Republican Party must eventually agree to become insiders. I am suggesting that in the long run the "above-party" solution will fail. The only possibility for the minority party to become the majority party is through a "party" solution—which none of the various wings of the party suggests. A party solution is one that attempts to strengthen party organization and develops a program for increasing the number of Republican Party identifiers.

This book has raised many more questions than it has answered. The student should speculate about possible answers to questions such as: What is the function of the minority party? Is it able to function effectively? Can a minority party in this political system plan to become the majority party? If so, how? What are the political effects of long periods of one-party dominance? Are frequent shifts between majority and minority status good for the political system? Are reforms in order? If so, should there be changes in the party system or in the constitutional system?

It is probably bad style to end a book with questions but it is my belief that in the study of political parties we have an abundance of poor answers and a lack of good questions. Students of American political parties should begin the tough assignment of framing good questions.

BIBLIOGRAPHY

Selected books and source materials for studying the Republican Party.

Party Histories

Agar, Herbert. *The Price of Union.* Boston: Houghton Mifflin, 1950.

Bartlett, R. J. *John C. Fremont and the Republican Party.* Columbus, Ohio: Ohio State University Press, 1931.

Binkley, Wilfred E. *American Political Parties: Their Natural History.* New York: Knopf, 1959.

Chambers, William N. *Political Parties in a New Nation.* New York: Oxford University Press, 1963.

Crandall, Andrew W. *Early History of the Republican Party, 1854–1856.* Gloucester, Mass.: P. Smith, 1960.

Curtis, Francis. *The Republican Party: A History of Its Fifty Years.* New York: Putnam, 1904.

Isely, J. A. *Horace Greeley and the Republican Party, 1853–1861.* Princeton: Princeton University Press, 1947.

Johnson, Donald B. *The Republican Party and Wendell Willkie.* Urbana, Ill.: University of Illinois Press, 1960.

Joyner, Conrad. *The Republican Dilemma.* Tucson: University of Arizona Press, 1963.

Kleeberg, Gordon S. *The Formation of the Republican Party as a National Political Organization.* New York: Moods Publishing, 1911.

Long, John D. (ed.) *The Republican Party: Its History, Principles, and Policies.* New York: M. W. Hazen, 1888.

Mayer, George H. *The Republican Party, 1854–1964.* New York: Oxford University Press, 1964.

Moos, Malcolm C. *The Republicans: A History of Their Party.* New York: Random House, 1956.

Myers, William S. *The Republican Party, A History.* New York: Appleton-Century-Crofts, 1931.

Republican National Committee. *History of the Republican Party.* Washington, D.C.: Republican National Committee, 1962.

Schnapper, Morris B. *Grand Old Party: The First Hundred Years of the Republican Party, A Pictorial History.* Washington, D. C.: Public Affairs Press, 1955.

Texts

Bone, Hugh A. *American Politics and Party System.* New York: McGraw-Hill, 1955.

Goodman, William. *The Two-Party System in the United States.* Princeton: Van Nostrand, 1964.

Greenstein, Fred. *The American Party System and the American People*. Englewood Cliffs, N.J.: Prentice-Hall, 1963.

Hinderaker, Ivan. *Party Politics*. New York: Holt, Rinehart & Winston, 1956.

Key, V. O., Jr. *Politics, Parties, and Pressure Groups*, 5th ed. New York: Crowell, 1964.

Leiserson, Avery. *Parties and Politics: An Institutional and Behavioral Approach*. New York: Knopf, 1958.

McDonald, Neil A. *The Study of Political Parties*. New York: Random House, 1955.

Penniman, Howard R. *Sait's American Parties and Elections*. New York: Appleton-Century-Crofts, 1948.

Ranney, Austin, and Willmoore Kendall. *Democracy and the American Party System*. New York: Harcourt, Brace & World, 1956.

Rossiter, Clinton. *Parties and Politics in America*. Ithaca, N. Y.: Cornell University Press, 1960.

Sorauf, Frank. *Political Parties in the American System*. Boston: Little, Brown, 1964.

Elections and Policy-Making

Abels, Jules. *Out of the Jaws of Victory*. New York: Holt, Rinehart & Winston, 1959.

Alexander, Herbert. *Financing the 1960 Election*. Princeton, N.J.: Citizen's Research Foundation, 1962.

Bain, Richard C. *Convention Decisions and Voting Records*. Washington, D.C.: The Brookings Institution, 1960.

Berelson, Bernard, *et al. Voting*. Chicago: University of Chicago Press, 1954.

Bone, Hugh A. *Party Committees and National Politics*. Seattle, Wash.: University of Washington Press, 1958.

Burns, James M. *The Deadlock of Democracy: Four-Party Politics in America*. Englewood Cliffs, N. J.: Prentice-Hall, 1963.

Campbell, Angus, *et al. The American Voter*. New York: Wiley, 1960.

————, *et al. The Voter Decides*. Evanston, Ill.: Row, Peterson, 1954.

Carney, Francis M., and H. Frank Way, Jr. *Politics, 1964*. Belmont, Calif.: Wadsworth, 1964.

Clapp, Charles. *The Congressman: His Work as He Sees It*. Washington, D.C.: The Brookings Institution, 1963.

Cotter, Cornelius, and Bernard C. Hennessy. *Politics Without Power: The National Party Committees*. New York: Atherton Press, 1964.

David, Paul, *et al. The Politics of National Party Conventions*. Washington, D.C.: The Brookings Institution, 1960.

————, (ed.) *The Presidential Election and Transition, 1960–1961*. Washington, D.C.: The Brookings Institution, 1961.

Fenno, Richard. *The President's Cabinet*. Cambridge, Mass.: Harvard University Press, 1959.

Galloway, George. *History of the House of Representatives*. New York: Crowell, 1961.

————. *The Legislative Process in Congress*. New York: Crowell, 1955.

Gross, Bertram. *The Legislative Struggle: A Study in Social Combat*. New York: McGraw-Hill, 1953.

Harris, Louis. *Is There a Republican Majority?* New York: Harper, 1954.

Heard, Alexander. *The Costs of Democracy*. Garden City, N.Y.: Doubleday Anchor Books, 1962.

Herring, Pendleton. *The Politics of Democracy*. New York: Holt, Rinehart & Winston, 1940.

Johnson, Walter. *How We Drafted Adlai Stevenson*. New York: Knopf, 1955.

Jones, Charles O. *Party and Policy-Making: The House Republican Policy Committee*. New Brunswick, N.J.: Rutgers University Press, 1965.

Kelley, Stanley, Jr. *Political Campaigning*. Washington, D.C.: The Brookings Institution, 1960.

————. *Professional Public Relations and Political Power*. Baltimore, Md.: Johns Hopkins University Press, 1956.

Key, V. O., Jr. *American State Politics*. New York: Knopf, 1956.

————. *Public Opinion and American Democracy*. New York: Knopf, 1961.

————. *Southern Politics*. New York: Knopf, 1949.

Koenig, Louis. *The Invisible Presidency*. New York: Holt, Rinehart & Winston, 1960.

Kraus, Sidney. *The Great Debates: Background, Perspective, Effects*. Bloomington, Ind.: Indiana University Press, 1962.

Lane, Robert E. *Political Life*. Glencoe, Ill.: The Free Press, 1959.

Lasswell, Harold. *Politics: Who Gets What, When, How*. New York: McGraw-Hill, 1936.

Lazarsfeld, Paul, *et al*. *The People's Choice*. New York: Duell, Sloan & Pearce, 1944.

Lipset, Seymour M. *Political Man*. Garden City, N.Y.: Doubleday, 1960.

Lubell, Samuel. *The Future of American Politics*. Garden City, N.Y.: Doubleday Anchor, 1956.

MacNeil, Neil. *Forge of Democracy: The House of Representatives*. New York: David McKay, 1963.

Matthews, Donald R. *U.S. Senators and Their World*. Chapel Hill, N.C.: University of North Carolina Press, 1960.

McCaffrey, Maurice. *Advertising Wins Elections: A Handbook of Political Advertising*. Minneapolis: Gilbert, 1962.

Milbrath, Lester. *The Washington Lobbyists*. Chicago: Rand McNally, 1963.

Moore, E. A. *A Catholic Runs for President: The Campaign of 1928.* New York: Ronald, 1956.

Moos, Malcolm. *Politics, Presidents and Coattails.* Baltimore, Md.: Johns Hopkins University Press, 1952.

_____, and Stephen Hess. *Hats in the Ring.* New York: Random House, 1960.

Neustadt, Richard. *Presidential Power.* New York: Wiley, 1960.

Ogden, Daniel, and Arthur Peterson. *Electing the President, 1964.* San Francisco: Chandler, 1964.

Peabody, Robert, and Nelson W. Polsby. (eds.) *New Perspectives on the House of Representatives.* Chicago: Rand McNally, 1963.

Penniman, Howard. *The American Political Process.* Princeton: Van Nostrand, 1962.

Polsby, Nelson W., and Aaron Wildavsky. *Presidential Elections: Strategies of American Electoral Politics.* New York: Scribner, 1964.

Pomper, Gerald. *Nominating the President: The Politics of Convention Choice.* Evanston, Ill.: Northwestern University Press, 1963.

Porter, Kirk H., and Donald B. Johnson. *National Party Platforms, 1840-1960.* Urbana, Ill.: University of Illinois Press, 1961.

Roseboom, Eugene H. *A History of Presidential Elections.* New York: Macmillan, 1957.

Rossiter, Clinton. *The American Presidency,* 2d ed. New York: Harcourt, Brace & World, 1960.

Scrammon, Richard. (ed.) *America Votes.* New York: Macmillan, 1956 and 1958; Pittsburgh: University of Pittsburgh Press, 1959.

Schattschneider, E. E. *Party Government.* New York: Holt, Rinehart & Winston, 1942.

_____. *The Semi-Sovereign People.* New York: Holt, Rinehart & Winston, 1960.

Stone, Irving. *They Also Ran.* Garden City, N.Y.: Doubleday, 1943.

Thomson, Charles. *Television and Presidential Politics.* Washington, D.C.: The Brookings Institution, 1956.

_____, and Francis Shattuck. *The 1956 Presidential Campaign.* Washington, D.C.: The Brookings Institution, 1960.

Tillett, Paul. (ed) *Inside Politics: The National Conventions, 1960.* Dobbs Ferry, N.Y.: Oceana, 1962.

Truman, David. *The Congressional Party: A Case Study.* New York: Wiley, 1959.

_____. *The Governmental Process.* New York: Knopf, 1951.

Turner, Julius. *Party and Constituency: Pressures on Congress.* Baltimore: Johns Hopkins University Press, 1951.

White, Theodore. *The Making of the President, 1960.* New York: Atheneum, 1961.

White, William S. *Citadel: The Story of the U.S. Senate.* New York: Harper, 1956.

Young, Roland. *The American Congress.* New York: Harper, 1958.

Zeigler, Harmon. *Interest Groups in American Society.* Englewood Cliffs, N.J.: Prentice-Hall, 1964.

Recent Books By and About Republicans

Adams, Sherman. *First-Hand Report.* New York: Harper, 1961.

Burdette, Franklin L. (ed.) *Readings for Republicans.* Dobbs Ferry, N.Y.: Oceana, 1960.

Curtis, Thomas. *87 Million Jobs: A Dynamic Program to End Unemployment.* New York: Duell, Sloan & Pearce, 1962.

Donovan, Robert J. *Eisenhower: The Inside Story.* New York: Harper, 1956.

Eisenhower, Dwight D. *Mandate for Change.* Garden City, N.Y.: Doubleday, 1963.

Goldwater, Barry M. *The Conscience of a Conservative.* New York: Hillman Books, 1960.

_____. *Why Not Victory?* New York: McGraw-Hill, 1962.

Gunther, John. *Eisenhower, The Man and the Symbol.* New York: Harper, 1952.

Harnsberger, Caroline T. *A Man of Courage: Robert A. Taft.* New York: Wilcox & Follett, 1952.

Hughes, Emmet J. *The Ordeal of Power.* New York: Dell Publishing, 1964.

Javits, Jacob K. *Order of Battle: A Republican's Call to Reason.* New York: Atheneum, 1964.

Laird, Melvin R. *A House Divided.* Chicago: Regnery, 1962.

Larson, Arthur. *A Republican Looks at His Party.* New York: Harper, 1956.

Martin, Joseph W., Jr. *My First Fifty Years in Politics.* New York: McGraw-Hill, 1960.

Mazo, Earl. *Richard Nixon: A Political and Personal Portrait.* New York: Harper, 1959.

Moley, Raymond. *The Republican Opportunity.* New York: Duell, Sloan & Pearce, 1962.

Morris, Joe A. *Nelson Rockefeller: A Biography.* New York: Harper, 1956.

Nixon, Richard M. *Six Crises.* Garden City, N.Y.: Doubleday, 1962.

_____. *The Challenges We Face.* New York: McGraw-Hill, 1960.

Pusey, Merlo J. *Eisenhower, The President.* New York: Macmillan, 1956.

Republican Committee on Program and Progress. *Decisions for a Better America.* Garden City, N.Y.: Doubleday, 1960.

Rockefeller, Nelson A. *The Future of Federalism.* Cambridge, Mass.: Harvard University Press, 1962.

Rovere, Richard. *The Eisenhower Years.* New York: Farrar, Straus, 1956.

Scott, Hugh D. *How To Go Into Politics.* New York: John Day, 1949.

Shadegg, Stephen. *Barry Goldwater: Freedom is His Flight Plan.* New York: Fleet, 1961.

Strauss, Lewis. *Men and Decisions.* Garden City, N.Y.: Doubleday, 1962.

Taft, Robert A. *A Foreign Policy for Americans.* Garden City, N.Y.: Doubleday, 1951.

Tower, John G. *A Program for Conservatives.* New York: Macfadden-Bartell, 1962.

White, William. *The Taft Story.* New York: Harper, 1954.

Republican Party Publications

Battle Line. Biweekly newsletter of the Republican National Committee (RNC).

Campus Republican. Newsletter published every two months during the academic year by the Young Republican National Federation.

Republican Congressional Committee Newsletter. Weekly newsletter of the Republican Congressional Committee.

Republican Report. Quarterly newsletter of the Arts and Sciences Division, RNC.

Southern Challenge. Monthly newsletter of the Southern Division, RNC.

The Republican Clubwoman. Monthly newsletter of the National Federation of Republican Women.

Young Republican National Federation Newsletter. Biweekly newsletter of the Young Republican National Federation.

Proceedings of the Republican National Conventions.

National Federation of Republican Women. *The Republican Clubwomen's Leadership Manual, 1962.*

Young Republican National Leadership Training Institute. *Young Republican Campaign Guide, 1962.*

The County GOP Leader's Manual.

The GOP Precinct Leader's Manual.

Republican Workers' Manual.